Encounters

∞

The Love and Sex Dance

Encounters is dedicated to Hope and Faith, with whom my encounters have been, perhaps, the most challenging.

Encounters

∞

The Love and Sex Dance

The Quest for Deep Sharing

Roger Golden Brown

Golden Galaxy Publications

Published by Golden Galaxy Publications
Copyright 2015 Roger Golden Brown
ISBN: 9798224376728

Please contact me if you have any questions.

I can be contacted at the following e-mail address:
wordsmith@goldengalaxies.net

Visit my personal website:
https://goldengalaxies.net/

And check out my world affairs oriented website:
https://goldengalaxies.net/Quasar/

This book is available for sale at:
https://books2read.com/encountersloveandsex

See all of my books at my Author Page:
http://books2read.com/rogergoldenbrown

Also by Roger Brown:

The Truth Seeker's Handbook
Themes of my Life
Reminders From Life for Life
Heading Out
Encounters
Insights
33 Years of Dreams

Foreword

For over 20 years I wrote in journals, expressing feelings, waxing philosophic, and following threads of thoughts and emotions that lead me sometimes to understanding and sometimes to deeper quandaries.

Of course, the search for love and the desire to be close to women led to many writings in my journals. This book is the retelling of my encounters with a number of women in real time, being made up of journal entries in chronological order. Each encounter in this book is generally a period of time chronicled in my journals; some spanning a very short period of time, others longer. Most begin with entries setting the stage, as to where I am at, before the encounter and continue after as I seek resolution.

They do not include the "girlfriends" of my life; the relationships of some duration. Nor do they include all the women I have touched or who have touched me. They are, although "limited" in their duration and depth, none the less, relationships in which personal emotional patterns did play a role and which offered me opportunities to act and react with an improved self and to refine my behavior.

I feel that this book is unique in that it is about a man's search for the highest love shared with a woman that is at once the highest love a person can feel. That means that all elements of spirituality, openness, and desires for the good of the giant family are in play.

As I prepare this book, rereading my writings as editor and publisher, I am amazed and perhaps even a little embarrassed by my openness back then because I have closed myself down some and such free expressions of love, desire, and affection, while still part of me, don't flow out as easily. And at times it seems excessively emotional, even as I honor the spirit in which it was written, the sincerity, and the ultimate truth of the importance of our expressing our feelings, whatever they may be.

Encounters

Prologue

These are encounters of the heart. Of this man's heart.

Some of these encounters are also encounters of the body. Of this man's body with a woman's body.

Although it seems certain that in every encounter our hearts touched, that which I carried away was my heart alone. My heart alone to feel and allow.

These encounters always have context. This is life. With every encounter with another being, there is a personal encounter with myself; with my life. Likewise each encounter sprang from my life.

It is my nature and has always been my way to have a probing mind. I value curiosity and fascination. I hope always to find value and, ultimately, resolution (albeit naturally temporary) in experience. If not resolution, harmony at least.

I have tended to allow my body and my emotions and my feelings to turn on to what is attractive (in the purest sense of the word) to me. This has often led me to unmapped territory where I must use my wits and wisdom, my ideals and values, my words and those of others, and sometimes some tears to guide me safely through.

To allow the heart to lead is fraught with danger. With beautiful danger. Everything is broken up and dances. There are risks.

A ship is safe as long as it stays in port.

But that's not what ships are built for.

Introduction

For me relationships have always been a stage for transformation.

My emotions are deeply connected with my whole body. My emotions are both cause and effect of my body's moods. Sex (and sexual desire) for me is never an experience isolated in my genitals. It touches every part of my body. In fact, I feel sexual desire more in my head and in my arms and in my chest. It affects my health and well-being. And often, when the openness is there, it affects the health and well being of those I share with. Love as a healing. Sexual love as a healing; and always as an opportunity.

An opportunity for myself and everyone involved to grow in truth. To allow the heart, which I believe knows only truth, to lead. And for me, when it comes to encounters of the heart, I don't think monogamy is possible. When the heart is open and love is welcomed; really truly welcomed, all love is fair game.

I believe that ultimately we all seek to become one, to break down the barriers and commune with one and other freely. I believe that our purpose on earth is to remove the obstacles to that communing.

We are cells of a greater body. But we have our own sovereignty. We have our own free will. The beauty of that sovereignty, though, is that it feels good, when harmony prevails.

In taking bodies and living on this plane, there are games that prevail that we are compelled to take part in. And there is the biology of the animal bodies we take.

I believe the innate desire to commune (and distaste for living as hermits) coupled with biological attractions compel us to take many personal risks and reach out in intimate relationships. Foremost are intimate physical and sexual relationships.

And this is a powerful and primary vehicle for us to learn about ourselves, to develop our confidence and personal power, and for us to learn how to treat the individuals who we engage in our most intimate and challenging relationships. Ultimately, to be better able to relate more personally with less friction with all beings.

For me, both the beauty and the complications of encounters with women have been timely - clearly each time being a reflection of where I'm at - and have offered opportunities to grow and deal with the next part of myself that is ready to be revealed to me; and hopefully matured.

I have chosen to limit or censure very little of my journal entries. An example would be the references to sexuality; whether real experiences or my fantasies and desires. Although there are probably sexual references which could have been cut out, I believe that one of the highest tools for growth is to validate all feelings. To face our lust, greed, doubts, fears... whatever; to listen to all of the voices. I have not added references to sex to make it more exciting, nor have I avoided any to make it more comfortable.

Also, it is interesting in reading my journal entries to note where my focus was. And how the most immediate things I wrote about may have differed from my later viewing the whole experience. And how all elements of my concerns in life interplay. It has often been true that sex, when I'm oh so hungry, seems the pinnacle of my quest, but once shared with another, I have written very little of it. Appreciation reigns... and then, at that point, my quest is one of the heart and one for understanding and harmony and togetherness.

I hope these pieces of my life read well. But that is not the purpose, ultimately. I hope that the reader can find pieces of themselves and their lives in my candid sharing, and hopefully be inspired. Certainly my style is my style. Perhaps, at times, readers will take exception with how I responded to or how I dealt with situations, with myself, or with others. Maybe this too can spark something of value within the reader. If it makes you think, or better yet, brings up feelings, that is good.

Beyond the personal (inter)play between individuals, there is also the society we live in. In my life I have always run into limitations and inhibitions that are primarily functions of buying the paradigms of society. Others will, for ever, try and put you in a neat little slot; in a box. Even more difficult to deal with, if one chooses to deal with it, is the fact that others have put themselves in boxes. I hope what I have written will occasionally challenge the reader's ideas of society or, perhaps, support their quest for a new day of social possibilities. One where humans following their hearts define society; instead of where we act within predetermined parameters of social rules carved in stone.

I would like, for a moment, to go back a couple of sentences. I wrote, "to deal with, if one chooses to deal with it." This is important. We have the choice to not deal with the complications of seeking harmony and understanding with others; to retreat and find solidarity in ourselves. Sometimes this is appropriate and necessary. Other times, and this goes back to what I said about the desire for contact compelling us, there is an agreement between parties to quest, and to struggle if need be, and to continue to deal with each other to seek solutions. Regardless of the choice, what is important is to not deny feelings, to not deny experiences, and to continue to deal with oneself to seek solutions.

It is a wonderful thing when encounters of the heart and encounters of the body are shared and there is agreement. It is a wonderful thing when encounters of the heart and encounters of the body satisfy our desires. It is a wonderful thing when such encounters help keep the wolf from the door. And when such encounters provide windows of opportunity for our soul's desire to commune and to seek harmony.

And finally, a note on the use of the word sleep as a euphemism for sex:

As a preface to these encounters I think it is important that I clarify some of the language I use. I often make references to "sleeping" with women or wanting to "sleep" with women. When I say sleeping, I mean sleeping. I find the idea of using the word sleeping to mean having sex to be an abuse of language that seems to come from a tepidness about talking about sex. It confuses things and kind of supersedes the incredible pleasure of spending a night with the company of someone by your side, irregardless of whether the two of you had sex or not. And when the word is used to mean sex that didn't even necessarily take place in a bed, it seems to kind of sterilize it. So, sleep means sleep.

For context, I think it is important that the age of the person, me, living and responding to these encounters should be known. I was born in 1950, so these encounters take place from the age of 26 until the age of 42.

Lazy Man's Guide To Enlightenment

Sarah, June, 1976

Prologue

I had been living in Bellingham, Washington. A friend of mine who lived in Olympia, told me he knew a man there, Gary, who was a carpenter who was looking for a partner. Having carpentry skills and liking the idea of working with one other person as a team, I got in touch with him, went down to Olympia, and we met and talked. It was a good connection and we decided to go for it.

He was ready to get started clearing some land and building a house in the woods on the Olympic peninsula, a couple hours drive from Olympia. It turned out to be a good partnership and very satisfying work.

I moved down there knowing only Gary and our mutual friend who had put us in touch. Gary lived on the outskirts of Olympia west of town. It was largely undeveloped, having woods and fields around his house, while being just three quarters of a mile from town.

I found a little cabin to rent some miles out in the country from Gary's. The cabin was very rustic. It was summer, which was good because the cabin was certainly not weather-tight. There was no running water to the cabin. It had a sink in the kitchen and outside the kitchen there was a structure which held a small water tank which needed to be filled by hand from time to time.

Visiting Gary, I got to know his household and their friends. He lived with 2 women in the house, both in their early 20's; Karrie and Sarah. And a man, Doug, who lived in a small room built into the back of the garage.

Olympia is situated at the southern-most point of the Puget Sound, where several inlets separate several peninsulas. Olympia was a college town and a few miles northwest of town, out on one of the peninsulas, was Evergreen State College, a pretty progressive college. It was a nice community.

Friends of Gary's house - Ken and Scott (a couple), tall silver tooth Mike, and John - were to become good friends. The Westside had many communal households that we got to know through our "food conspiracy", a collective for buying food in bulk. The houses all had names. Ours was Budilnik, a name Gary took from a character in a story. Another was named Kallyope, whose people I got to know well.

It was summer and life was good.

Olympia, Washington

June 27

I hardly know what to say or how to say it, dear journal. Today has been a beautiful day.

I'm at Gary's, writing this now. It's 11:30ish. Really warm in the house. Ken reading. Me writing. All others in bed.

I rode - beautifully - to town. It felt really good. I arrived here to find Sarah the only body home. We talked a bit then went off on our bikes to Fraser pond. My first swim of the year. Beautiful, to be sure. We swam, touched, held, played, smiled, talked, toweled each other off. Together.

We rode home (I say "home." This house - Gary and Sarah's - feels like home to me.) and ate a Ken and Scott dinner. Beethoven's 6th Symphony (the Pastoral) and lying and being close to Sarah for desert.

Followed by Gary and Scott playing recorders. A very beautiful day.

Final thought. It felt a little odd being the one of six men in the house to be close to Sarah tonight. But it felt better than it felt odd.

June 28

I slept over on the floor at Gary and Sarah's.

Sarah and I took a bike ride up to Priest Point Park then north and east into the country.

We split a beer and I felt loose and we talked and touched in a field.

At times today there were uncertain vibes between Sarah and myself and at other times we held each other warmly.

In her room, just before I left, we had a short talk. I tried to explain that I dug our relationship but it was hard for me to turn off my sexual energy and my "I never want to let go" energy and I hoped she would realize this is all new to me. And I have to learn how to co-exist... Well shit. I'm getting lost in words. To make a long story short, we seemed to reach an understanding that pleased us both. We held and touched each other outside beautifully as I departed.

There's lots more I could say but I'll just say - something new has come my way and it's beautiful.

June 29

Home now. My home. It's still, quiet. I'm mildly depressed. It's really hard for me to believe what I know. About Sarah's and my relationship. That we will probably be closer and further apart on different days.

Today we talked some, did little together, touched very little. When we did it was me mostly initiating it. Like a day without my fix, I felt (feel) all wrong not being held tightly and in the many ways of the two previous days.

Of all the women I have known, Sarah touched me in more beautiful, sensuous, and warm ways than I have ever experienced before.

Shit, I am depressed. Why, oh, why can't I relax and accept things as they are.

Well, I guess I'm here to learn.

I feel now like one of those moods where I wish I could cry, release, and follow with the necessary philosophy. Perhaps if I keep writing and thinking I will get together a philosophical outlet.

On another subject, I had a fascinating experience today. I took off on a brisk bike ride, a smiling Sarah saying she likes my hairless face because she could see my smile, sending me off. While doing laundry on the hill I was feeling really good. I met the guy who lives there. A middle age long hair. Really nice guy. It got me so high I had to release. I ran, jumped, clapped hands, and yelled a bit outside.

Upon returning I talked to Sarah. I told her of my experience. She cautioned me about being too high. I kind of think that really got me onto my depression trip.

Since Sarah's and my swimming expedition I have been fairly tense. I've been totally relaxed and high when we're together and when I'm feeling good about her. But when I'm doubting our closeness or when I've been at her place waiting for her to come home I've been restless.

Sunday Sarah and I swam, laid in the grass, and laid together to the Pastoral. Monday we rode, talked, and touched in incredible ways before my ride home.

Tuesday, now, I feel - somewhat - alone, empty.

Think asshole, of the beauty of that woman, of the time we had together. That's still there. Today was just different. That's all. Get your fucking self together!

Today's highlight - Trying to get myself together.

"I let my woman flow to her own natural rhythm."

"I let my woman flow to her own natural rhyme."

I've got to. If I don't I'm a fool.

June 30

Lake Cushman, Olympic Peninsula.

Good timing has put me in the woods to mellow out.

Three women, two men here as company. Good folks.

It's beautiful here. A very beautiful evening. I'm very high in a very slow peaceful way. Just what I needed after my very highs in excited fashions.

Most of the evening's talk was to the tune of drizzle, fire, and seemingly unending twilight.

I don't think I need to be overly cautious of being too high as Sarah cautioned. Rather I just needed to move into a high of a different kind. From a different source and of a different energy level.

It keeps the high full that way.

The Love and Sex Dance

I'm surrounded with so many good generous people. I only hope I can play at least at par. I must learn to give. Certainly I believe I'm giving, but it must become natural.

July 4

Back home now.

I'm really depressed. I don't even know why. Perhaps giving up in my mind the idea that Sarah is a companion. Still a friend but I feel no close vibes. Shortest relationship I've ever had. Whatever that means. Looking in her eyes I felt that there were more close moments in our future. I never did feel a boy-friend, girl-friend relationship, but I guess, without even thinking about it, I expected some sort of continuing growing thing.

I'm not really sure if Sarah is the cause of my depression tonight but it seems like it must be. My depression is kind of undefined but I kind of think it's extreme loneliness. The loss of what I thought was to be - a future of warm touching, tight holding, and maybe even kissing which we only began to get around to.

Something that I think I haven't said in my journal in a while is that I really wish I had a girlfriend. I think a lot of my feelings about myself and Sarah stem from the fact that I desire more than just the high of being close at times. I really feel the need for a woman to "come home to." I really would like that feeling; waking up next to a woman.

But I guess that's something I just can't rush. I can only hope that somewhere in the future that the right woman and the right me come together.

Times like this, I feel extremely weak. Maybe not though. "People who need people are the luckiest people in the world." But I have people. Just not a girl-friend.

I sure wish I wasn't sleeping alone.

July 11

Love is the key word. Today there are two highlights. I will write of the 2nd one first. I read the Lazy Man's Guide To Enlightenment tonight. My feelings before picking it up had been easy going; I was ready for it. I won't write of it, too much, just that love is the key and its manifestations in all actions.

One thing that set it up was sharing smiles, eye contact, and warm embraces (and a little waltzing) with Sarah this evening and (the all important and) going with the feelings like music. Letting one note go by to hear the next. Love again.

Before reading the Lazy Man's Guide I felt like declaring Walt Whitman love and passion to her and expressing that I would (sometime - when the experience might feel beautiful to us both) very much like to sleep by her side and to make love to her. But as events would have it the moment of my expression wasn't today. She, Mike, Holly and John, Ken and Scott, and Gary went to watch the fireworks. I trailed slowly behind and returned straight away to the book.

One reason that I trailed slowly behind tonight is that I was subdued by the most (I think) major injury of my life. Alone, at my place, isolated in the woods, filling my water tank, I fell back off the boxes I was standing on that I had piled up to reach it. It was also the worst fall (I think) I've ever had. I fell straight backwards in the debris, and taking stock of myself, amazed I hadn't really gotten bashed, bruised, head smashed, or broken, I noted a huge gash between my thumb and pointer finger. Guts and fleshy innards exposed. In a flurry of adrenaline rush and reason, I repiled the boxes, climbed back up on them to my only source of water and washed it, tied and tightened a sock around it, (expecting gushing blood loss), tried my phone to find it dead, then took off in my car towards town. I stopped to go back to Kim and Claudia's to use their phone in hopes of finding a doctor close by. No luck so off to St. Lukes but now knowing there was almost no blood loss. I relaxed and took it in stride. I watched my hand get sewn back together. Five stitches. Lotsa bandage wrap. What a trip.

The climbing, instability, and fall seem like interesting metaphors. Sarah's caution to not be too high. And the fall leading to my reading Lazy Man's Guide To Enlightenment. Also the repiling of the crates and climbing in clarity to wash it off with the only water available.

Well, it brought me into Olympia so I stopped in, in time for dinner, at Gary and Sarah's. Being here again is kind of strange. I love (that word again) these people so much. I love Gary strongly in the way I love men and I do love Sarah in the way I love women and I love them both as people. Equals in the universe. I don't want to live alone now. I am sure.

I desire to let my love grow for and because of people (lovers) around me.

Not much else to write.

Love.

July 12

I feel now that touching and holding Sarah, as this morning, is becoming better as I realize when the time is right. She sensed before a kind of desperate need of mine to touch her and it wasn't right. Now, I know, I can enjoy each note, letting it go, to hear the next.

July 27

To Pachelbel's Canon again (which has become my music of these days), I feel at peace.

Tonight Sarah and I shared much close vibes. After the house meeting disintegrated quietly to the tune of Robert Frost, while saying a good night to Sarah, including the first real kiss of any depth we've shared, I asked her if she would like to sleep together.

She said not tonight; that there would be time. She also said that she was confused. I was touched by her saying what she said and the way she said it. I felt very close. As if we were vocalizing things we have previously communicated only through touch (or the lack of it).

Anyway, I don't want to analyze the shit out of it. Just that things grow. All things change. My feelings (love) change and grow (not always up) for her. I feel mellowed enough for the first time today to feel totalove.

Well, actually the people here made me feel quite warmly welcome during the meeting. A good start.

Now I must continue.

July 28

I had planned all day today to talk to Sarah. Hopefully to soften her confusion and to learn more of how she feels.

Words sent beautiful feelings.
She inwardly awkwardly learning inside - something new.
Me expressing - do it in your own time - my love.
Us desiring, but waiting.
Hold, kiss (slowly), hug (tightly).
Smiles too (serenely and yes; truly).
"Good night" ... "Good night" ...
Door closes. She in. Me out.
My name. Her voice.
I turn, door opens, she comes.
"I love you."
"I love you too, Sarah."
Arms around each other.

July 30

Today certainly has been a remarkable day. Mostly just to mention that Sarah and I made love today. Afternoon Delight. In the back yard. Almost stupid to write it. I doubt if I'll forget it. Nice. Yes, nice.

When I'm without, it all seems so bizarre and foreign but when I do make love after a long fast it just feels so normal, natural, and right. And good.

A lot of what I felt today was good feelings that the time was right and that Sarah enjoyed it.

I expect that for both of us there will be some new feelings and head trips to explore. I feel that our relationship has changed. But I feel that I have to mostly relax and continue to feel the love I have felt (grow and change) for her for so long.

Well, in time.

August 5

A many feeling day:

- Good morning feelings.

- I rode with Sarah to school. Me feeling like I was reaching. Desperate almost. Mellowed a bit, as I re-felt us.

- I asked her if she would like to sleep at my place. Instant cold reaction - decision later.

- Me riding home alone. Feeling so much a need for a female companion.

- Sarah (just after a long phone talk with Bill; her, I guess, boyfriend back East who she had never mentioned) on the phone a long time with Paige. Me listening. Sarah talking of relationships, of needs, of it hurts not to be close, of all things pass.

- Myself thrust into a head trip, gut emotional, high. Beethoven's Pastoral from the backyard outside speaker, trying to clear muddle. I had some success but mostly only really started feeling good to the tune of Sarah and John's (a fine friend - I love him) company to the 5th movement.

Softening then through a musical collage of single cuts.

Now, I feel ok but I know that under my surface feelings I strongly desire to hold, touch, lie close to, sleep with, and make love to Sarah.

I really feel that another woman who I felt good about would also be very nice although Sarah is special.

In any case I'm just plain tired of sleeping alone, of unfulfilled sexual desire, of being lonely.

I am beautiful - though sometimes when lonely I feel I have nothing to offer.

Sarah is beautiful - though sometimes when our vibes don't match, she seems (my head) hard to me.

Gary is beautiful - most all the time.

John is beautiful - a fine friend. He likes me and makes me feel good.

Karrie is beautiful - though seldom here, she is good company. We have had some open talk.

Doug is beautiful - extremely generous and unfortunately not here anymore.

Mike is beautiful - I know why Sarah likes him. I do too. Caring, sensitive vibes. Slow walking and peaceful harp.

Sigrid, Lisa, Sue, Ken, Scott, the Kallyope folks, more...

Beauty abounds.

Yet I still get lonely. I guess I just need people. To be physically with. Bad? Good? Who knows? I do know that it feels great and it hurts.

I'll just plug along and try to be good. Try to exude totalove as much as I can in any mood.

I wish I wasn't sleeping alone.

Final Note: Love

August 30

Tonight for the fist time since I met her I had that feeling of wish I had never met this person - it would have been so much easier. Such a weak attitude. Not for the first time since I met her, I feel like I wish I could cry just to flush out this pressure in my head. Too much thought; when I should relax. We'll talk again. She's beautiful and understanding. Whenever we talk (about things) I feel good. Regardless, it seems, if the cause of the need to say things is resolved. Well, actually that's not true. Things really are resolved. The true nature of things is unveiled from immediate emotional needs. Wow what a special person in my life.

Hang in there Brown. Love yourself. I do, but still it hurts.

Fall

September 7

This, I found in my journal, must be Sarah's writing:

"Early morning - low mist, and the neighbors birds are carrying on as usual. Roger and I biked down to petersins for some last minute tripe. It will be a while before I see his back rising like a lighthouse over his khaki casted flanks. I remember the last time I left behind his behind in the tacoma terminal. Um. His shoulders give me faith in the strength of individuals and in man's ability to keep his LOVE alive."

October 3

Sarah has gone home; back East for I don't know how long.

You know, it's funny how when you fall in love with somebody you kind of learn to count on them for a certain amount of your happiness. It's funny how just seeing them walk in the door or how coming home to them in the house can make you feel so good. How just riding a bike beside them can feel so much better than if it were anybody else.

I really do miss Sarah. Today I'm not thinking of kisses, of sleeping together, of making love, or really even of words said. Just how nice it was when she was around just being Sarah.

I kind of feel like so much of my potential for happiness was her presence in my life. Sure I know that there are other avenues ahead and that there are other loves ahead and that time will bring much to me - but - I miss Sarah.

Lately I have been waking up each day with an empty day ahead, searching for one event after the other to fill up the time. It's so much nicer when you wake up and the day unfolds in front of you.

Midwinter

January 1,1977

The snow falls evenly.

The fire crackles erratically.

I might as well be at the ocean for all of nature's rhythms. So comfortable. To be a part of those rhythms. To vibrate independently - sort of.

Much heavy thoughts of old age, death and the futility of life as I near the end of reading Earth Abides. I know (or feel) that to be happy; not to worry, and to go on is the lesson... but now - it weighs heavily.

10 more pages.

Fuck man - sad - I don't know what else to say.

I want to say I wish I had a wife. But she could die also. I don't know if I could survive the Great Loneliness. I want such a crutch so bad but what if it is removed after learning to rely on it.

Epilogue

After discovering in mid August that Sarah had a boyfriend back home, and after meeting him once, I didn't write much more about us. He was a really heavy un-nice man who she had some long ongoing thing with and, I guess, I was just an affair. Truly an affair of the heart, though. What we had was something she could never have shared with him. Now that I knew what it was that she hadn't been able to share with me, our relationship changed from being a close / not close dance to me wanting to offer her an alternative to the obnoxious man. But it wasn't in the stars. We were always on good terms but us was over.

Metaphysical Rebirth

Nancy, May, 1980

Prologue

For the first time in seven years, the previous fall, I had chosen to move into a big city for a while. It had been a lonely winter. I met Joanne late in the winter and we spent much time together all spring as friends, as pals. She was young, beautiful, graceful. Dancing was her life. Fear of failure was her nemesis. I was in love with her. She was in love with dancing. Her loneliness seemed to be some obscure and incalculable part of her equation. She was so sweet and genuine. I wanted her. I wanted her as a lover. I loved her as a friend. And... she turned me on. I wanted to show her what love could be... she didn't need to be lonely. Compelled by my own loneliness and desire, my ongoing unrequited suggestions of more intimacy might have easily driven a female friend away, but she actively sought out my companionship time and time again. Once or twice we dabbled with physical intimacy. Her body was open while "she" was not into it. We were each other's best friend all spring.

Come late spring, she was making plans to go back East - home. Another dear friend, the woman who had drawn me to Seattle in the first place, was also leaving. And I had had enough of big city life anyway.

Seattle, Washington

May 8

I felt really bummed out today. I was feeling a little bitter about my relationship with Joanne. And feeling that aside from getting along so well there is something inside Joanne that I feel is really her that I'm in love with. But also feeling surprised at myself that I haven't gotten tired of the surface Joanne. Surprised I'm so attracted to a woman who gives so much of her power away. And who feels so little sexuality. Though I know underneath she is very passionate. And I'm surprised at my attraction in spite of how unfree she is.

I guess the problem is I feel so sure that I know more than she does how beautiful and free she is underneath her problems, cares, and social crap.

God would I love to make love with a free, loving, wanting Joanne. She is an incredible kisser. She is so sensitive.

May 18

I was sorry to find out tonight from Joanne that she was super bummed out. She'd had a bad weekend. But I felt good because I think she is near being forced to change. At least I hope that's the way it will go. She is too good. I hope she can help herself out soon. Funny, but I always become very sexually aroused when she talks about how fucked up she is. I think it's strong feelings of caring and affection. I guess combined with my sexual longing.

Mt. St. Helens blew its top today.

May 27

My sexual frustration is reaching a new peak. Everywhere I look I see female bodies. TV, advertising, magazines, everywhere. I see couples happily enjoying each other.

I wandered around the Folk Life festival today. It just depressed me. Later, I ran into Joanne and her friend Andrea and Andrea's friend John at the Cause Celebrè Cafe; Andrea and John touching and caressing each other.

Planning to come home then go to the dance, I picked up the flute and it was magical. I played two hours nonstop in front of the fire. Best ever. I felt really high.

Then I went off to the dance. I had a nice talk with Barbara. And a good talk with Virginia. I also felt mutual attraction with several other women. They were all with other men.

I left feeling shitty. Home now. To bed alone. It bums me out. Since talking with Sigrid Friday about positive attitude I have been rebounding each day - many times. The weekend has been absolutely shitty weather (it's been gray and drizzly for two weeks now) but I have been trying to remain positive. But there are limits. Sure I met some nice people tonight. That is positive. It's all part of growth. But I'll never see them again.

Just to say I desperately want sex. I would love to make love with a woman with a beautiful slim body - and God I hate sleeping alone.

May 28

After a weekend of intense sexual frustration - a change.

Many subtle things this past week have combined - it seems - to make me feel like changing myself. Talking with John in the sauna. Talking with Mary this morning about astral projection. Starting reading The Philosopher's Stone. And maybe mostly - a certain amount of positive spiritual influence from Sigrid and time with her. She is a beautiful woman.

So today I just decided to glow. To vibrate. I felt good. I had a good day working - even though things fucked up. I took a walk on the Ave., glowing.

I touched more today and it felt good. I smiled lots. I shared good vibes and words with Becky; guitar player singer at the Cause Celebrè. And I had a good time with Dana.

Home alone - now - feels fine. I know it's all coming my way. "Who in the hell d'you think you are? A super star? Well, right you are!"

May 30

I'm keeping my spirits up - I'm really trying. I had a nice short talk with Sigrid. I really would love to make love with her. I'm sure it would be easy to love her, to touch her beautifully.

Home alone late I felt lonely. But ok.

Evening at brother Doug's house.

Today I drove up to Bellingham. I'm sure I want to move up here.

The Big City is fucked. Streets are hard, people are hard. Even the beautiful, warm people in Seattle seem so much harder. Here in Bellingham I feel so comfortable. People dress relaxed. They walk relaxed. In a few hours here I have seen more beautiful women than in a week in the city. Men too. Many more smiles.

Upon arriving in town, I drove down the alley to Doug's house and saw a lightly clothed woman in the new sun weeding her garden.

After unpacking my car I simply walked up the alley and started a conversation. I helped her weed. We made a date for some food together tomorrow and maybe recorder flute duets. She is attractive to me. I think she's single. Her name is Nancy.

I'm really feeling like I am making it happen for me. I need to smile. I need to be forward and bold beautifully. To do what I want. Try and meet who I want. Any words will do if I glow enough.

I didn't feel frustrated today but I did fantasize the wonders of sex.

If I keep glowing like the last few days it seems certain a woman will share sex with me soon. Everything else is heightened also. I shared good vibes with Ken today.

June 1

I visited Nancy last night. We talked for a long time. We touched for a long time. As the hour long radio shows flowed by we made love for a long time. She is a wonderful lover. It seems so easy. We shared simultaneous orgasms. Pretty fancy stuff, huh.

I had to sleep alone though, because she felt awkward about having me stay because of her kids (Gabe and Israel). Too bad but it's ok. I really like her kids and they like me.

Playing with magnetic letters on the fridge yesterday, they were piling all over me. Nice. I felt like a dad.

Tonight I spent the evening with Nancy again. She enjoys touching all of my body and uses all of hers doing it. Very sensuous. Very peaceful. Very passionate. She looked really good to me tonight when I first saw her. She touches wonderfully.

It feels a little odd that we're not sleeping together but not bad.

Well, since I decided to be positive, life has been beautiful for me. I smile lots. If I catch my self forgetting, I smile right away. I have a beautiful lover. I expressed myself wonderfully to Steve.

I feel all right.

June 2

I spent another evening with Nancy after dinner. I made my best ever frapple pie. With grape-nuts and top layer of pear. Nice - very nice - parting moments tonight. It felt - feels good.

June 4

I'm back in Seattle.

I just had a really nice visit with Joanne.

She confessed she's been feeling really empty lately. Numbed. I care for her so much, it hurts me. She talked about it a bit then we snuggled on the couch. She drifted asleep. It felt good to be able to relax and assure her. After being a little down this afternoon I turned my thoughts, while she was resting her head on my chest and relaxing, to positive feelings of caring for her and what a beautiful person she is. That felt good.

June 5

Bussing home today, I smiled and talked with a really attractive bus driver. She is a long distance runner. She was obviously attracted to me. At the end of the route we smiled and said goodbye. I walked a few steps and looked back. She was watching me. We smiled again and waved.

All day I've been feeling so high. Almost too high. I need to keep my feet on the ground. I feel so charismatic, bold, outgoing. I think I'll ride the bus with her tomorrow.

I feel like if I leave Seattle now I will never know how the city would be for me if I continued to glow as I am. All things seem in order. Things fit.

I feel fine but still wish I had a lover tonight. I think more of my bus driver friend than Amy, who I met at Mary's. I'm turned on by a woman giving me a second look.

June 11

I'm back in Bellingham. I drove back up yesterday.

I dreamt this powerful dream this morning.

I was standing behind a fence backstop watching a softball game. I was with somebody - maybe Stadler. A softball and a couple of players went right through the fence a few times. I figured they could do it because they did it spontaneously. Later I, and I think Stadler, talked about it and tried to do it - pass through the fence or a wall - I forget. I was very high. It seems kind of like on pot. I approached a wall and stood nose and body touching it. I got into a really high vibratory state - shimmering. I pushed a little and I began to mesh with the wall. I pushed a little more and slowly slipped through the wall. What a rush! Mike was excited. It was too intense for me to do right away again. I explained to him that you simply had to be high enough then wait until you sensed the right rapport. We knew now that it could be done and looked forward to more experimenting.

When I awoke I was sorry to discover it was a dream.

June 12

Morning now. A little tired. Listless. I made love with and slept with Nancy. I feel a little odd about it. I'm holding back a little; knowing she's a Christian and feeling that.

I've been very high lately. Maybe it's time to try and use some of my latent mental powers. Some thoughts:

From The Philosopher's Stone: Relax and expand.

From Beethoven's Symphony #6 cover; Sir Donald Francis Tovey on Beethoven: "has the enormous strength of someone who knows how to relax."

I visited Barb (ex-girlfiend) yesterday. She said she felt nervous in my presence. It seemed to me she was nervous in the presence of my calm. I feel like she gives away her power. She said things weren't going that well but it was ok. That validating of her okness but not having what it takes to go further was always one of the biggest difficulties for me in our relationship. I think it's fine that people think they are ok because we are all superstars but I also think it's good to feel and admit when things are wrong. Enough to decide to use your own power to make changes.

June 14

Last night I went to Nancy's and hung a while with her and her friend Ted. I'm not quite sure what is going on between them. I don't think Ted is her boyfriend; he's doting on her and wants much more from her than she does from him. Nancy was whirling around cleaning. Nancy asked Ted to leave because he was just hanging around in the kitchen. I asked her if she wanted to be alone. She said she was just into cleaning - that's all. Later she came up to me and softly asked me to stay.

We slept together. Last night and also this morning while we went second hand shopping together she was very affectionate. We didn't make love, which I wanted, but still it feels nice to be wanted.

I felt that Ted felt bad. I think it's hard for him.

This morning I dreamt of Nancy and I and Ted. Nancy and I and several others rented a house. Ted, I think. There were different scenes of the house. Scenes of a kitchen.

Next, I was near Little Bread Company in Seattle. In the dream it was a food co-op and I went in to stock up. Nancy was there with her mother. There were strange scenes of two men having a hard time sliding something.

Finally I'm walking along; almost to a new house. Then, in a hallway I passed a room. There is a man at the door. Nancy is inside on the phone dressed in something provocative. Lounging. The room is his bedroom. I make small talk with him, sneaking looks at Nancy. I was feeling hurt but trying not to show it; knowing it showed though. I walked down to the house telling myself she's not mine - it's ok - I shouldn't feel possessive, knowing it's not really that but I am feeling very hurt.

Nancy told me this morning she had a flying dream and it told her tonight she should go out alone. Or maybe with women.

June 15

This evening, I played Parcheesi with Lynette, Scott, and Nancy. Nancy was being very affectionate. Sometimes it's hard for me. I want her more. I want more sex. But I don't want to expect too much. Nancy is very attractive to me and I do love her but I don't want to feel that it is more - no - different than two beautiful people coming together at times. That sounds so nice. Yes, it is. But needs and wants can't be ignored.

June 16

It was an interesting emotional night with Nancy tonight. She cried. She talked about her son and his father's relationship not being good.

We shared some close moments. She told me she wanted to sleep alone but she thought she might regret sending me off. I tried to talk her out of it. I started to leave, then turned around, walked back to her and into an incredible hug. I came back in for a few minutes. We joked about it. I said what if I just walked up and got in her bed. She said she didn't know. I lifted her on my back and carried her around to lock doors and turn off lights. And up the stairs.

She was in a weird mood and said she didn't want my last impression of the day of her to be weird. I assured her I knew her better than that. She laid over me and hugged me. Sort of uncomfortable for me but I let her drift off. When I moved her, she thanked me for letting her drift off and went back to sleep.

It was nice to sleep together. I had strong desire for sex (and still do) but that's ok. (Sort of)

June 18

I'm back in Seattle. I'm still working on orchestrating my move to Bellingham.

I'm kind of lonely tonight. I think of those beautiful moments when Nancy would just come up to me and hug me last week. And I love the way she watches me walk away until I'm out of sight; a very nice feeling.

June 20

Bellingham

I feel blown out, hurt, lonely; letting myself feel my emotions. A chance to find out if I can rebound and feel beautiful and positive again soon. I really don't feel I have it in me now.

When I got to town I went to visit Nancy. She wasn't home. I met her and the kid's on my way to Rawls to buy a paper. Iz and Gabe calling "hi Roger" and running up to me. Nice. Nancy was in a quiet reflective mood.

We went back to her house.

She told me Ted wanted to live together with her, that they were lovers, and she was being kind of depressed by trying to decide. She said she was feeling it was probably not the best because she was resisting.

It was my turn to feel hurt and envious. I went into the living room, maybe to cry, and laid on the floor. She came in quietly and caressed me for a while. Then we went and watched the sunset. I was feeling fine, vibrant. After momentarily, earlier, feeling there was no more reason to move here, I felt it was all positive and we will have our times together.

But later Ted came over. I let them talk and Ted left in a while. She asked me to leave after she had wandered around in an emotional daze for a while. She also asked me not to come over tomorrow. When we parted her hug and touch had no substance. That felt strange.

I was in tears ten feet from her door. She watched me till I was out of sight. I cried in a lump in the alley for a while. Then I dressed warmer and cried and walked around town.

As I wandered around town in the after midnight hours, I saw houses with lights still on and asked, "Why are you still up tonight?" "Are you hurting too?" "What's your story?" "Do you have what you want tonight?" It seemed there must be so much loneliness in the world.

I wonder why I cry tonight. The same reason a baby cries. Nobody has touched me the way Nancy does or looked into my eyes the way she does in a long, long time.

I think if she didn't have another lover I would be content to be close to her when it was right for her. But now the emotions and the unsureness all around is so unstable.

I feel so lonely. And I feel like a hug and attention from Nancy is the only cure. But... I think I know better.

Earlier tonight Gabe came up to me and asked me if I was looking for a house. He said he wanted me to show him Doug's house tomorrow. Then he said if I found a house, maybe if it was close they could come and visit. He's a beautiful kid. I love him. Then he said if it was farther maybe I could take them out there sometimes. He asked if he could visit the first day. I said it might be busy and he said he could help unload. He may be only a kid but still he was a human being expressing affection for me openly and desiring my company and attention. It felt great.

I do love Nancy and I hunger for her touch and her attention. The way she is so sensitive to my moods. The way she watches me leave. The way she makes love with me. Though it's been a long time and that hurts too.

Tomorrow is a brand new day.

June 21

Quite an interesting sleep. A thread of thought all night about Nancy. Many dreams about catching a glimpse of her today. Some dream about a door to or of our love opening and me being aware of the colors of light coming through the door as it opened and thinking about the significance of the colors. About how they signified the change. I think I remember a soft red mostly.

June 24

Nancy and I slept together and made love last night. She wasn't completely into it. She said she wanted to explain something to me. But she couldn't do it. She doesn't say a lot of what's going on in her mind and it's hard for her.

She is beautiful.

Bed now - I've been thinking a lot about last night. How I need to talk with Nancy. To tell her how I feel I wish she would tell me more of her wants and needs. So when I'm with her I can act in a way that will be more comfortable to her.

I felt she was uncomfortable last night, though she was also silly and somewhat playful.

June 30

I just got totally weirded out by Nancy. Yesterday we talked about maybe dinner today. I went over and after not saying what she meant, she told me she didn't like being around me. Didn't like my attitude. It was really weird.

She doesn't say what she means. She has a hard time explaining her feelings. I feel vindictive now and maybe I'm being bitter but I don't think she tries very hard. I think she puts things off - doesn't face them.

I know I used to be that way. But this is different. Maybe I have been weird to her lately. Because I have been struggling to be sociable; trying to figure out why all of a sudden she doesn't seem to like any thing about me. Just last week, at the movie she was so affectionate.

I am sorry to have any relationship end on a sour note. But I'm afraid this one just has. I'm afraid it has to be up to her to come to me, if ever, and I'm skeptical.

I almost feel like crying, but I feel too bitter. I really honestly feel she is at fault. And that I have tried. Unless I made the mistake of misunderstanding how hard of a time she has with what to me are situations and to her problems.

The Love and Sex Dance

I think she takes my boldness and openness for arrogance. I'm sorry but I can't change those qualities, Nancy. They're beautiful and positive.

A little while later -
Nancy came over shortly after I left her house. We had a long, long talk. Too much and not enough was said. I felt mostly like I guess I just didn't really know her as well as I thought. I really believe what we had when our quiet peaceful sides came together was beautiful and real. But I guess there are many parts of us that are radically different. I'm truly sorry she can't handle visits without it being weird. Nuff said.

Cept I'm sorry. I really am.

July 14
I called Nancy today, answering her call of yesterday. I had offered to baby sit for her. I thought that might have been why she called. She said she had just called because she wanted to touch me. I told her she was welcome to call me for that anytime. She was kind of down. Overdosed on motherness, she said. I look forward to seeing her when the time is right.

July 15
I've finally succeeded in moving to Bellingham. I love my new home with Donna and NancyW. It's so nice to be living with two women who are becoming good friends. I really enjoy NancyW's company. I like the way she moves. Physically and otherwise. Donna is a very positive, healthy woman.

In Seattle, I lived with three women but this is so different. None of my Seattle roommates were attractive to me physically and very little spiritually. My roommates here are young, vital, positive, attractive women.

July 16

I had many weird dreams last night. All about social sexual frustration. I was bummed out about women who are afraid of men wanting them sexually. Sex is such a wonderful, beautiful, fun thing. Why so much fear? Why not happy to be attractive and to be wanted? I'd give anything to have women want me.

One dream of being with Mary, my kissing unanswered, on a plateau in Bellingham with a Mt. Rainier view and wanting her to come with me and climb this exceptional peak above the plateau.

One with Anita in line with me somewhere. Two men make advances at her and she has her choice. I start yelling about how unfair it is. I realize I'm making a scene but continue.

One where I'm skimming down a fast river passing a house on the shore with available looking women on the porches over the water. But I encounter a dog at one house and am afraid. I pull up and wake up.

July 20

Out of this summer, that's been virtually void of sunny days and summer warmth, today broke a stretch of cool gray days. It's warmed up this afternoon and it's beautiful, but I'm bummed. I've been longing for summery weather, but now that it's happened I almost can't stand it. It's so much harder to have a sunny sexless day. My whole body aches with sexual desire. I feel like screaming, pounding, quitting. I just gotta be bold and beautiful and if I make somebody uncomfortable I'm sorry they don't see it as a beautiful wonderful thing.

Where do I have to go to find women who openly enjoy sex for itself; for closeness and love for their own sake? It's so beautiful and fun and people deny it to themselves because it scares them.

People are so afraid.

Off on my bike now.

Later -

Life is a trip.

I rode bike to Tarzana Falls, Whatcom Falls, then up Yew Street to Lake Padden, in search of a meetable woman.

I passed a woman at a private little beach, exchanged hellos and smiles. I walked on aways, then convinced myself to go back.

I sat with her and talked. It was nice. Her name is Denise. We swam, talked, laughed together for a couple of hours. She is very attractive to me in many ways. She has an incredibly beautiful body. And clear green eyes that looked into mine for long moments that seemed both innocent and bold. But probably were neither. Just her.

We had dinner at her house. During a long held look I said, "let's make love." She was surprised but not really disturbed. No, she wouldn't feel comfortable. I told her she was very attractive to me and she said I was to her.

She put on a low light and we sat against a pillow on the floor for a while. What a nice time.

Now - home - alone - I should feel good and do but I also feel very frustrated. Waiting. Shades of meeting Joanne. And still the very strong desire for sex. And for snuggling, closeness.

And... physically she is one of the most beautiful women I've ever been close to.

And... she leaves town in three weeks. Strange how life never brings anything simple my way. But it's my life so why should it.

I found a piece of paper on the ground today at Tarzana Falls. It said:

The worlds not what it
seems to be -
Why do we take it
seriously

July 21
Morning warmth. One of only four or five such days this summer. Beautiful. Beethoven's Pastoral Symphony sounding good.

Warm but distant memories of Denise's presence. Her eyes and humor.

But my sexual desire is so strong. I would gladly make love with another woman less attractive to me than her, if I have the chance.

It is such a shame that it's so hard to have something so wonderful.

The Love and Sex Dance

When I feel frustrated with how much reserve women feel about sexual relationships I think of Mary and Sharon. The two women in my life that love freely and without fear.

Pastoral music carrying thoughts fluidly with so much more grace than when I opened up this book to complain that I wanted to be inside a woman.

Now my mind is washed with warm thoughts. How much I would like to hug Sharon, then slip through the hills and hug John.

Love and affection..

I feel so much. The pen is so soft.

This is summer. White shirt shade warmth.

Pastoral music. I wish they would broadcast it from the top of Sehome Hill.

Wouldn't it be nice.

If we could say goodnight and stay together.

Breathe deep. Inhale the mood.

The enormous strength of someone who knows how to relax.

Sometimes everything seems so available. I'm certain that really in not so much time I will be satisfied. But... that feeling has yet to prove true.

Final thought as Beethoven relaxes. I am a little overwhelmed at how beautiful Denise is to me.

Twilight -

Too much to write it all down - all the lyrics of Help. No... the entire album side.

I went up to Lake Padden to discover two of NancyW's friends, Stanley and Rod, were sitting with Denise. Denise touching Rod, the way I was wishing she would touch me last night.

We shared one of her incredible looks but I had a hard time sparkling, like last night. I felt a little envious but mostly just added lonely to my feelings of the day.

I know she is attracted to me and I do feel good about it. We will have some time together but it does hurt.

I feel like crying.

Now, playing Joan Armatrading. This time a year ago I listened to this while touching Mary lovingly.

I feel so much!!!

Oh well. I'll go with my mood tonight. I feel beautiful; just lonely. (With a lover I could hold my head back and really laugh.) God, what feeling, Joan.

I do look forward to seeing Denise Wednesday. She seems extremely clear and centered. Quietly sure.

I've been in Bellingham ten days and at least my loneliness seems so much richer. I guess that's good.

Today it's mid 80's for the first time since April. Setting sun behind broken clouds gold and moon behind broken clouds silver. Shimmering lace beauty. It's 12:30 AM now and still 70°. Even the grass is warm underfoot.

Tears.

You know it seems all the warm sensitive men I know are always wishing they had a woman to be affectionate to. Someone to share love with and bed with. How do women find the strength to sleep alone. (maybe not fair, there's more to it than that) It is just so undesirable to me.

I think about the way I touched Denise's face last night. Even though my touch wasn't returned she didn't shy away and wasn't afraid. I feel glad that I reached out and expressed the affection I have to give.

Now - Thuille's Sextet is sounding beautifully mellow. Wish I could be caressing someone to the caresses of this fine music.

Epilogue

Nancy and I were never lovers again. But after a time of not seeking each other out we bumped into each other one day, and resumed our friendship. We spent some time together, went out together sometimes. Once or twice we slept together as fellow cuddlers appreciating the warmth of another body and the heart of a friend. Ours was an understanding of having survived some awkwardness, and a desire to acknowledge the natural chemistry we had together and had initially shared so intimately. A good basis for a friendship.

The day, May 28,1980, was the day that was to be referred to by me as my "Metaphysical Rebirth." After earlier years of my life being full of psychic and cosmic magic, I guess I had been a little asleep for some years in my quest for the "right" woman. From that day on, my hunger for spiritual truth could never be separated from any other quest or any other compelling desires or circumstances.

I have continued to be in touch, now and again, with Nancy. For me, among all else that she was, she was the woman I first made love with two days after my metaphysical rebirth and our first time coming together was the day after I wrote, "I'm really feeling like I am making it happen for me. I need to smile. I need to be forward and bold beautifully. To do what I want. Try and meet who I want. Any words will do if I glow enough. If I keep glowing like the last few days it seems certain a woman will share sex with me soon."

Whole Earth Fair

Boehr, April, 1982

Santa Cruz, California

April 15

I finished reading Bioenergetics (by Alexander Lowen) last night. I really like what he said near the end about principles. How you can't intellectualize them. They come from feeling. Feeling that certain ways of behaving or acting feel ease-ier. More frictionless. More harmonious than others.

I'm marking many passages that seem to enable me to use my mind to understand my body. It's something I feel I need because my mind has corrupted my body so much up to now. For example the idea of de-crystallizing positions or attitudes that had their place in growth but now hinder openness and flexibility.

Such as me saying I won't fall in love, having decided that it was usually such an isolated act coming from having one connection as an outlet for Totalove. But now I'm feeling that the fall is good.

Everything I learn and feel these days, Reich - Shankara - Pundit Acharya - Lowen, says feel, don't think. It would be really something to be able to feel fully enough, to love from feel, to develop principles from feel which I could live and be comfortable with mind as a tool. As Cayce says, "Mind is the builder."

Now - what can I do about it? Reading these inspiring books helps me know or guess what to do. But they don't do it. I need to try and be fearless in putting myself in feeling situations. A hard hard thing to do. Decrystallize my attitudes and get out there.

April 22

I feel that this phase is a growth period of radically repositioning myself. God, I hope so. But I'm not sure if I'm trying enough. As I write that, though, a realization. Is this just what I want; not trying, but being; and learning to feel and be differently?

April 23

I'm thinking back to how many times sleeping with lovers I was aware of how my breaths would often be one to each two of theirs. Mine would be long sighing exhales, pause, then deep filling. I never do that sleeping alone. I always go to sleep tight.

I must become more into feeling emotional vibratory contact with people around me; with friends. Talk less small (mental) talk and let feelings free themselves. It seems we, as people, need some kind of communication when we are together. Perhaps touching - usually only with lovers - is communication enough. Sharing. And an opportunity to feel and exchange life energy.

April 30

I had this dream this morning:

I was about 60 feet above a pond on a tower platform with several others. One man was throwing something off. I was about to climb down when people started wiggling around. I fell off and into full flight down. I was concerned but not afraid. I got into the wind blowing by my face. I flashed on maybe I like wind because it reminds me of falling. Finally I went into a dive position and went into the water. I went to the bottom and stuck in the mud. Mild panic and struggle, then I tried breathing water. It worked. So I breathed water until I was free. I surfaced, then tried walking on the water. Another success.

I got into walking all around; just trucking on water.

Some touristy looking old ladies came by and also walked on the water. I discovered there was a rubber tarp over the water.

The dream and its feelings started to fade as I peeled up the rubber and, I think, still stood on the water.

(Synopsis of May Day weekend. Not a journal entry.)

Friday, Saturday (May Day), and Sunday I spent in Davis, California for the Davis Whole Earth Fair. Over the course of the 3 days, I met a woman from Davis, Sarah, and spent the nights with her as lovers. And I played hacky sack with a woman, Boehr, who I knew vaguely from Santa Cruz and finally got to know her. We made a really nice connection and would come together back in Santa Cruz. And I met a woman named Jane from Chico who I felt a real attraction to. I told her I was planning to go up to Washington, my home turf, in a few weeks to visit friends and we made vague plans for me to stop by and visit her on the way. She was going to be going off to Canada with her family for the summer but maybe I could go up before she left.

Strangely, I didn't write anything in my journals during or for several days after the fair. Maybe it is because I was so alive and in the moment.

May 6

I just read another chapter in Illusions. What Sarah said and what Richard Bach is saying move me to strengthen my awareness of my need to do what I feel. Not worrying about how it will all fit together, or how I will get it all done, but knowing, really knowing that if I do what I really want, life will unfold smoothly.

I can foresee making decisions about time that will put me through periods when it's hard to remain true to that philosophy. But, God, if I can come back to it; really try not to waste time in between decisions, wandering. Wandering physically is fine, so long as I am moving myself through a space that's where I want to be.

And what do I want now? I just played through an old one: I feel bad that I may experience rhythm because I have something to look forward to: my next communication with Sarah. Then I thought. So what. It's ok. If it's good time for me, then fine. If I have to face a change later, that's ok. Let it be later.

And thanks to Jane for your loving perceptions of how it's all how you look at it. There are no standards for events. Only how it is for you when it is.

May 13

Getting together with Boehr back here after getting to know each other at the Fair has evolved. I spent last night with her. Warm water bed, head trips, and Seabright Avenue traffic kept me up for a while. It gave me the opportunity to watch Boehr sleep though. She looked so peaceful.

We spent an hour softly together in bed this morning. Velvet skin, round shapes, softly twinkling eyes.

I had this dream last night: I dreamt that I was dancing with light weight golden chains all around my body. I learned how to move so all the different tones played a song.

May 14

You know I want to say this: I love Sarah. I love Boehr. I find myself feeling this and being afraid it's an ego trip: hey, I've got 2 lovers. But it really isn't. It scares me that it could be but I know what I know.

I asked Boehr how she felt about me going up to Davis this weekend to see Sarah; as good as I feel about Boehr right now I need to see how Sarah and I are together. She said it was fine. And that I wasn't choosing or rating. She is such a beautiful whole woman.

Sarah and Boehr; you are both so good for me and to me. I can't thank you enough.

May 17

I spent the weekend in Davis; most of 48 hours with Sarah. We really got to know each other and Saturday we had a couple of pretty intense discussions about our different beliefs. She's is so skeptical of my spiritual path and I can't just say well, ok, it's just a belief. I feel it too much.

But we had a wonderful Sunday. We softened ourselves and truly enjoyed being together. We watched beautiful blue, black, and white long tailed birds, climbed a short tree and smelled its exotic flowers, swam in the river. We never made love but were affectionate a lot and occasionally passionate, we hacky-sacked and frizbeed, and covered a lot of ground on our bikes. We went to a garage sale, a potluck, and a hardware store, and showered together.

Our goodbye seemed really nice. Warm, touching, and I think a balanced feeling of knowing our differences and knowing our bond and affection.

I do love her.

Wonderings - scared sometimes that this can't continue. But I know better. More growth periods, for sure. But my heart is true. And I feel my love flowing. I hope that never stops. I don't know how it could.

It feels so good.

May 18

I feel like I'm into a phase of struggling right now. I feel my love slower and more poorly expressed.

I saw Boehr today. It felt good but I felt that it wasn't as easy as last week. But still humor with her seems easy. She is so beautiful. How she talks and how easily she listens. She is a wonderful woman. I'm happy. But even that feeling doesn't seem to include all of me or as much as it did last week.

The weekend with Sarah was such a growth from pure romance to getting along being together a lot and helping take care of each other. God, maybe I am ready. Ready to share myself with someone else.

Actually, it would be kind of amazing if I don't feel more in the way of getting used to my new situations in life. Two women who really care for me.

I feel, as I write that, I wish I could cry. The fullness of feeling. I am trying, trying to love and happily I'm finding myself with people who love and share love.

May 22

I went over to Boehr's last night. It was a nice time of sharing thoughts and feelings about who or what we really are.

We slept together. We made love for a long time. Being close to her is so nice. Just caressing the endless soft curves of her body feels so good.

I feel so lucky and am fascinated by the qualities of Sarah and Boehr and how they fit into my life.

As I write this, though, I am aware that I need to be sensitive to the fact that I am also in their lives and should be open to caring how my qualities can be helpful and complimentary to their lives.

May 23

I've been reading Pundit Acharya (Breath, Sleep, the Heart, and Life) for a couple of weeks. It's full of many fascinating ideas, lots of words of warning and many exercises.

Through it all he says: Turn off the mind. And learn to be aware and feel how thoughts excite the heart and your breath and your whole muscular and fluid systems and glands and eyes.

"When you do use the mind learn to do it with a smile and sense of play and rhythm so your system has ease and rhythm."

The more I read the Pundit the more I feel it. It would be good for me to take time to practice his methods and to be aware and integrate ease into my active life. Eliminate or minimize jerky motions. Or, if I do move jerkily like playing hacky sack (even there, I can search for the flow) - take time to achieve an ease afterwards. Yes, as long as I can remember, I have appreciated that quality in myself and in others. It reminds me of Shane - the essence of Shane was fluidity of motion.

There is some quiet growth and ease in my life giving hope through these still somewhat awkward days.

May 28

I went and visited Boehr. There was a lot of distance between us for a while. But we got to talking. She is overwhelmed by too many people wanting her. One ex-lover, another friend who wants to be a lover and she doesn't, and many dear friends who want to spend time with her, and me who would love to be close with her often.

I feel now, for the first time, that some of what's so hard is how much I felt we had to offer and I'm sorry that the growing the way we were is no more. We talked about psychic influences. I sort of apologized for hanging on. I can't believe how hard it is for me to release her.

MacArthur Park is melting in the dark...

I left there in a warm dreamy state. Feeling beautiful and graceful. My only 5 hours sleep last night is making me slow but not too tired.

All the sweet, green icing flowing down...

So I guess I need to accept the situation is that this just isn't the time for Boehr and I to be really focused on each other.

Someone left the cake out in the rain...

Stroking Boehr's body gently I really felt gentle evenness all around her. She is so warm and sincere.

I don't think that I can take it...

Hoping - (yeah, I know) to hear from Sarah. But somehow it seems that this time is not going to be easy.

'Cause it took so long to bake it...

What wonderful life Sarah would be to reassure this struggling soul. I remember her so many strokes. "Such a good looking man." Oh god.

And I'll never have that recipe again.

Freedom is the lesson we must learn.

I just am in disbelief of how hard it is for me to release Boehr. And myself.

On a positive note (well, actually it's all so positive) I called Chico yesterday. Jane wasn't there. Her roommate Annalisa was so nice on the phone. She said that even if I couldn't somehow make it by Jane's leaving time, that I should come visit her, for sure. So much love.

I feel myself about to burst with emotion.

How do all these things fit? Raw emotion, spiritual self, free choice. Awareness of growth, happiness. Balanced emotions - feeling centered but aware of a range of emotions. Well, I just don't know. Cause they just aren't fitting.

May 30, 1982

Some thoughts about choice. In my dream the other night I realized - hey, this is a dream - I can do anything I want - I'll fly. Last night, lying in bed, I realized - hey, this is life, I can do anything I want today, feeling good, giving, and my heart. I'm thinking about my struggling times the last couple of weeks, how I was aware all the time that I could change if I wanted to; how I chose those moods. I wanted to feel those ways. I really did. It's a fine line between choosing to feel low to feel it to learn and choosing to lift oneself high.

June 5, 1982

It is the full moon today. And I am also responding to yesterday's deep tissue session with Fateh working on the my groin area.

The feeling started growing a couple of hours ago and has reached frustration. Part of me feels balanced and happy with my life but I do, I really do want sexual sharing. I feel like being with Boehr and just telling and touching her I want to touch and kiss and open and expand with her.

I feel incomplete. I feel so so much I want to be with a woman. Tonight. It feels like it's totally wrong for me to be alone. I don't know how else I could put it in words. I feel incomplete; feel it in my heart. Not my poetic heart but right there. Center - core - in my chest.

I'm lonely.

I want a lover who is a playmate.

I want a playmate who is a lover.

Thinking earlier how much time Mary gave me. She really did.

Full moon. I guess I got those full feelings.

The Love and Sex Dance

June 7,1982

I don't know why I didn't say it to Boehr yesterday when I saw her at the dance at the Civic Center - a little healthy anger might have been good - but I was really disappointed. We had said we would call each other Saturday about getting together Sunday and she didn't seem to remember. Maybe it would be healthy for me to express that to her.

Today I went to Boehr with the intention of expressing my anger/disappointment. About her saying things that create expectations, and feelings of togetherness that she seems to forget. I also wanted to ask what changed. Sure I know her time is tight but that's not all. These are things I've accepted into myself stoically and this morning when I awoke it was clear to me that it's unhealthy. I want to talk mostly for me but I also feel it's good for her to know how she affects one who she is close to.

It's hard for me to be angry but it feels so much like it's right and good.

I told her it was hard for me. She reminded me that she wanted me to feel free to come to her if I needed to express something. She was so wonderful. We talked a long time. She really really wanted to be clear and to help me feel good and really tried to tell me how things changed.

She also convinced me how much she does care for me. She told me that last night at the Civic Center watching me dance and move about, she found herself wondering about how warm and sensitive and what a nice person I am and why we're not being more together. And not coming up with any reason.

Tears came to my eyes. I really feel in a different time we could grow closely so wonderfully together.

She said it was her that changed mostly and my vibrating at a lower level and/or moods and growth periods (all my words) didn't affect her caring.

I just couldn't leave without knowing for sure so I said I wanted to stay and make love with her. I was feeling so much soft loving affection for her. So tender. She said no; it didn't feel right.

I think I'm going to feel better about it. About her. I kind of expect that it'll still be hard until she leaves on her trip. But, God do I feel good that I won't spend the summer holding ill feelings toward Boehr.

I've never felt so beautiful about my sexual energy as I do now; as I have these last few days. It feels so much a part of my vitality. I want to share it.

June 9

My life again feels positive. I feel open outward again. I can offer more outside myself.

It feels like my talk with Boehr Monday was the turning point. It's like I think about it and I can't tell what changed. It wasn't a philosophical outlook; a new acceptance. I just feel different. More at peace. I guess I cleansed some potential "barb wire entanglements." And I'm feeling that philosophy might be adversity's sweet milk but it invalidates the pain which wants to be acknowledged and released, expended.

I'm learning and I love it.

Epilogue

On my trip up to Chico I stopped and visited Sarah. I'm not sure how equal it was but I don't think the passion was ever really there. We wrapped things up to the extent that, although we liked each other, not enough to travel for it.

My letting go of Boehr was unparalleledly the cleanest in my history of relationships up until then and as clean as any ever, thanks to my knowing I had to honestly express my feelings and her welcoming me and meaning it.

Boehr goes. Love stays. Jane arrives. No more on Jane here as she doesn't fit into the parameters of an Encounter, as she was so much more; perhaps the deepest love of my life. We began when I was on a special high when I met or got to know three women in one weekend at a fair. And the work of my own and help from others helped keep the love alive and leave me open enough for something so special to blossom.

Sex With a Friend

Bari, November, 1985

Santa Cruz, California

November 23

I feel sad. Claudia and Rusty came up to my room to visit me. Claudia said don't be sad and came over and kissed me. She has so much love to give. And giving to love.

Looking at my U.S.A. for Africa record sleeve, people are starving, struggling. And I have such unlimited potential to heal this world and what do I do. I'm pitifully incapable of taking care of myself. A struggling soul.

Gordon Lightfoot sounded great.

A good sauna with Fred and Laurie was ok.

I played two hours of hacky sack with Rusty.

But shit, I long incredibly for the tenderness of unafraid loving. And someone willing to receive my emotionally involved loving without fear.

I've been reading Max Heindel's Occult Principles of Health and Healing. I feel so inspired to consecrate my body and nurture my vehicle for active and vital thought and action.

But will tomorrow be the same? I feel I must have something to look forward to.

Shit.

Music For Airports is divine.

Steady rain sounds wonderful.

It's reasonably warm.

Joel is depressed.

Rick is restless and desires a lover so much.

Claudia and Rusty are happy as clams.

I cried tonight. And thought some of Edi, Garalinda, Klemens, Traudl, and Johanna; my friends in Europe, now so far away.

It's insane.

No; it's an easy simple flow.

I'm insane.

Good Night.

November 24

Stoned now.

Thinking how when I'm stoned I feel more autonomous, and loneliness - lack of woman or lack of inclusion with All - is somewhat distant - and appeased - sort of - or delayed. Delays are not denials. No, delays are denials, in a sense. If it's not happening now, it never is.

November 26

Bari called me up last night. She recently moved into a place just a short walk from here. She talked in a positive mood about reaching out. I said I'd come and visit soon.

Later I called back and asked if I could come and visit right now. She said sure.

I had a wonderful moonlit walk over there through the woods. Peaceful and breathing.

So Bari and I talked of how we fear and screw it - let's love. Let's reach out whether we get rejected by others' fear or not.

We cuddled and eventually made love. Bari was silly and playful. And child-like.

I wondered if I could match her enthusiasm and discarded my fear. We were really silly and honest.

A bit of a surprise, though not entirely. It really felt wonderful to be so velvety and soft.

So once again I have a physical side satisfied (more or less) in a good sharing way, yet not feeling such a falling or that kind of chemistry.

Bari talked of being the observer, yet not sure of when and how to be involved.

I feel we both nurtured each other pretty well without trying much, naturally.

Bari and I talked on the phone this evening, both of us appreciative. She had a high day with people loving throughout, as did I. Curious how, of a sudden, there is an opening for us.

December 1

I spent last night with Bari again. We were pretty playful. And it was pretty easy. Sometimes I would feel myself not getting enough of something and/or wanting my space. Which is also defined a lot these days by loner habits.

We drew for a while. I was just fiddling with crayons and talking. She felt really disconnected and the vibes got weird. She told me about it and I just said hey, things changed. So what. We still like each other. I explained the possible ways to treat it and that there needn't be so much drama.

We got light and playful again.

We were sexual which I sort of enjoyed and sort of didn't. I feel our styles are different. I also feel a little less peaceful richness in our intimacy than I seem to want.

I really enjoyed the sleep. I slept great and it was nice to feel her shape, velvety skin, and warmth.

She really loved it. And she really wanted me. She just called and asked me not to go south and to stay and sleep with her again tonight.

I feel I'm very good for her. I'm being honest and not freaking or withdrawing (much) at the mood changes. She really needs and appreciates someone who will be present and help her understand her feelings of being suddenly disconnected from people.

It's an interesting combination of enjoying her, caring for her, not being in love, and feeling it to show her what levels of openness she can have.

December 3

I was so alive today. I went around downtown doing things with Laurie. I bought a Vaughn Williams tape. Fantasia on a Theme of Thomas Tallis and some beautiful stuff new to me.

I was so turned on by cats and trees and lawns and humans and the fairly blue sky. I was just laying back and taking it in. God it felt, and to some extent, feels nice.

Later -

I went to see the film Wetherby with Bari. It pushed her buttons. Interesting how, when we were talking afterwards, I felt the vibration of futility and loneliness. I really kind of felt myself believing in it until I recognized it as her energy. Bari really changes the energy in a place fast sometimes.

We talked in my car for a long time. I was really inspired and tiraded on truth and honesty and giving and receiving being pure in and of themselves, not needing a balance. It's the honesty of the act that gives the balance.

I had a really nice realization a few weeks ago that when one can fully receive, free of any implications; just take it, then you know; really know, what giving is and that it's worth it.

I felt that Bari and I parted after bringing the convo to a pretty positive and appreciative place. I feel myself in such a role of being a door to the universe to this bright young person, questing intently for purpose and unity.

December 7

My mind is feeling so fertile. I have this feeling, that now that I'm relaxing out of my slump, I'm drawing on such a wealth of wisdom. I feel that my newest tapes are such clear connections to unbiased reality. No grudge reality. The reality of I have enough problems myself without having anything against anyone else.

I've been continuing to be a happy observer of nature's nuances, easily taking in the subtleties as I pass through time and over the earth.

I'm so free of the grind in my head.

December 11

It's interesting to re-read my old journals and see the same patterns. For example, just being how I want and saying what I want with women who I don't know, I fear awkwardness. Today I felt such longing again.

I saw Emerald Forest with Bari last night. I enjoyed it, but I wasn't so overwhelmed by it, like I was the first time I saw it.

I was disturbed by some people behind us talking. After the movie I mentioned it to Bari and she said I should have been able to just ignore them; be with the movie and let them go. It pushed my buttons. We debated a long time. I'm sorry I dragged our discussion on.

It's interesting to observe my rationales for not being intimate with her. It's simply not the best chemistry. But that's enough. I don't need excuses.

I will call her now and apologize.

Wonderful ease of no grudge held. Yes.

December 13

2:30 A.M.

Awake - by the fire, just restoked for writing.

Dante and I went to the Harkle Road party. I was in a somber mood. I feel very sad. Because of, I think, watching all those free bubbly young people and feeling my loneliness and self-imposed pressure on my life's accomplishments.

I almost left many times but hung on. I met a woman named Michelle who was very attractive to me. And I got to know better and appreciated Rebecca. I massaged her a while. I felt so much desire to be giving so much physical love. Talking of feelings, she said how nice it feels to make love. She is so round and voluptuous.

I wanted so much to take her aside and offer to spend the night together. But she was just talking her sex; not suggesting anything to me.

She and Michelle and others were so free in the loving shared by all. Which seemed to make me that much more down on myself for wanting a specific sharing; not content with (though I was loving it incredibly) all the beauty all around.

Karl, Marisa, Ben, Bart, Royce, Lisa, Eric, Karen, Sam, Jim, Mark, and on and on. So many inspired, incredibly loving world citizens.

God, I'm lonely. I don't understand it. I don't get it. I do and I don't.

Talk with Dante reminded and re-inspired me to strengthen myself and prepare to heal and help.

Elton John was the special music that really turned me on, finally got me moving and dancing with all my heart and soul - Rocket Man.

Yes, I did open up and gain for it all.

Royce and I shared melancholy. That was nice.

My God.

So much love.

Stephen and I shared with each other how much we both felt we had been Walt Whitman or knew him.

I want a lover. A companion.

Bari and I talked a little more about the other night. Nothing but good and apologies for ourselves. We keep it clear. Leaving next to nothing to forgive. Beautiful.

Oh God.

Good Night.

Good Night, lovers.

December 21

I feel again high and loving. Rick invited me to go to a Solstice Gathering at the Grandview house. Wonderful people. A wonderful circle, vibrations, and words. Doug was especially beautiful.

Classical music has been really sounding divine to me lately. I'm enjoying the increase in inspired choral music on the radio as Christmas nears.

At one point tonight, looking around the circle, I was impressed by the inner beauty of all these people. And I reflected on how often I'm compelled by sexual desire and wondered why I fall (it seemed, at the time, like a fall) into that narrow focus.

I don't know.

I really don't know.

It sure is a big one for me.

December 23

I've been thinking of how going on the road - now and my summer going to Europe fantasy - is an escape for me. In a way running from my seeming inability to be as open as I want to be while living a normally aligned lifestyle. I keep pioneer spirit alive better on the road.

Yes it's an escape, but then what isn't. We live in such a field of forces that to align ourselves and live within our environment is indeed facing a higher responsibility. No, not like guilt responsible. Like co-operation responsible. Nature gives us the ultimate show of randomness and order in such a blend. Go with strengths. Be on the road, if that is where my power is.

It was a crazy day today. I had too many plans. All this drama is no doubt because normal life is too boring for me. So I go on the road in my mind if not in my senses and body.

December 25

I'm continuing to feel so far from patient. I don't seem to be able to relax enough to read, to write letters, to play flute, to take a walk.

It's incredible how much I feel the desire, the need for a woman. Perhaps, related to my thoughts on travel, I feel that that need is not a weakness but knowing it's the most effective way to live among certain forces in this body, at my particular stage of development, to enhance my power.

I don't know.

I have so much appreciation for what Bari gave me. For a couple of weeks, I felt I had given and received with such purpose, shared intimately. I was calm.

Friends and Sex

Christine, February, 1986

Santa Cruz, California

February 1

Last night unfolded in such an unexpected way.

I showered and shampooed my hair. I felt all clean and fresh.

I called Suzanne and she wasn't interested in going out.

I called Heidi for company. Maybe eat some ice cream. She wasn't home.

I saw Christine's name on my phone list and called her spontaneously.

She asked what I was doing. I said I was tired, should sleep, but I was a little lonely and probably would go out. She said she was a little lonely too. I said how about if I bring some ice cream over. She said she didn't want to eat, but come over for tea.

So I got there and I felt free and she felt like a good friend. KHIP played country dumb music and I loved it. She was beautiful and so was I. She held hands with me while we talked and when she took her hand away to reach for something she replaced it with the other before she broke contact, as if to let me know she wasn't pulling away.

We had a conversation about friends and sex. How it should be possible to love a friend sexually and not lose them. We agreed.

She said something about how much she hated sleeping alone. Always. I said let's sleep together.

It was all such a strong feeling of two mature adults expressing their feelings. So different than with young women. I realized how much I need that more than the enthusiasm and ideals of youth.

She said no, she can't. She couldn't sleep with me without making love, she's too sexual.

I said so, let's make love, whichever. I told her she had already been wonderful in her friendship, smiles, and contact alleviating some loneliness and it would be wonderful to give her love.

It was: well it would feel nice, smile, but... friends and sex.

We touched and held each other a lot. She ran her hands through my hair and caressed me. I caressed her. I felt my head against her body. I lightly touched her breasts.

It was velvet. It was the first time I've felt velvet in so long. It was divine. It was over as soon as it began.

Leaving, I stumbled across the street, tears already coming. I cried in my car for a half hour before I could conceive of driving. I've hardly ever heard myself moan and ache so much. It was strange.

I drove home at 20-25 mph. Still, it was barely safe, I was crying so hard. Dream gliding up Branciforte, I multiple yawned several times. George Winston's music seemed to bypass my ears and go straight to my brain center feeling the sound, affecting me.

I cried on and off till almost 2:00. Almost two hours. I was stunned. I just don't get it. I feel like I'm being punished. It's so ludicrous. Twilight Zone.

Still, I feel no sense of rejection. It was a wonderful experience. And I know I must continue in the attitude I decided to adopt yesterday; to consciously decide to be happy. Maybe (I'm not sure) I've brought out enough from my gut to be happy in spite of the often challenging results of being tenacious and risk taking. The affection Christine and I shared is evidence of a harmony, not a defeat.

So... onward, though it all seems so futile sometimes. Cruel and unusual punishment.

Later -

Today my heart has been so open all day. Fred called again this morning just to say he was thinking about me and that our time together yesterday felt special.

I'm listening to On The Threshold of a Dream. I did so twice yesterday, really feeling it.

I went to the Harkle Road house to tape I'm on Fire. It has rained intensely for three days and today is mild, patchy blue. I really don't know if Santa Cruz has ever looked so alive and exotic to me. Runners, skaters, surfers, skateboarders, bikes, color, hair, vibrant people. Beautiful men. Beautiful women ripping my heart.

I'm in Logos' parking lot. As I wrote that a beautiful woman walked past. To her it's just the body she inhabits. Watching her, I feel heaven in my heart. God, I'm freaking out. My love is burning like a forest fire.

Karl was beautiful. Changes with Michelle, Bart, and Marisa (tears now) and genuine care for my condition. I feel better about him and Michelle, having asked him. Marisa gave me a hug that made me not want to leave. It felt like we were lovers or ought to be.

I have not let go of Marisa's hug yet. Wow. I've been talking with people a lot. Sharing life's passion with many. I am again fully alive. Deep sharing flowing.

I feel like I am doing well. But. I still don't feel good. I'm still in a kind of desperate agony. Maybe it's just that now I've decided to go down in a flashing radiant light of glory, instead of in some dark alley.

1:30 AM. Final note of the day. I feel free. Out of college, money spent. See no future, pay no rent. Oh, that magic feeling. Nowhere to go.

I am not satisfied. But I am pursuing my heart. Again, I'm so alive and giving so much to people. Nudging confidence into their lives.

"The difference between me and you, I won't argue right or wrong, but I have time to cry."

February 2

I visited Christine today. We talked some. Then we went to Pergalisi's and drank tea. She was very affectionate. We held hands and walked arms around. It felt really nice to have a touching female companion. When she touches, it is very firm. She's really there. I like it.

Curious. I don't feel very romantic and don't wish to be her boyfriend. But I feel there is an energy of lovers. Just without sex. I think she enjoys the man; just has it in her head to not make love.

February 7

I feel great. I'm a believer.

I'm at home. Alone. I just got a ride home from wonderful Greg, who has recently become aware of his pilgrimage.

Some notes on exercise and confidence.

Yesterday I ran a couple of miles, then sweated at Kiva. I ran into Clover. Beautiful. We exchanged phone numbers. What a smile and gentle penetrating eyes. I felt great leaving there.

Today I rode to Cabrillo and back with Tafay. And played hacky-sack there. I had fun. I really did.

Hacky-sack was magic. I felt sharp and playful.

I called Janey and pushed for a massage trade. Firm in my desire and confident in its goodness.

I called Christine and loved her voice and laugh. She said yeah, let's do something interesting for your birthday tomorrow. I really like her.

I feel solid and beautiful, into creative communication and spontaneous adventure in human contact. It seems so significant that I unravel the mystery of these perfect, god-given relationships.

Two springs ago I learned confidence.

Last spring a new level of confidence crystallized, which prepared me for my trek to and quest in Europe last summer.

And again I learn (relearn - why did I forget?) - the hard way - through trials- to get back to the power of Confidence.

- - -

God, I heal everyone I touch; everyone I'm close to, everyone I even think of, so much more, effectively, beautifully, easily, when a lover is close. I want a lover - a woman who can help me shine.

Will I ever finish? (Whatever that means.) Must my physical world always remain as ethereal as my spiritual progress?

Try and stay with what you know in the heart of your heart. To not do so, out of fear or for manipulation is to lose some self respect and to give power to the game. I don't mean manipulating others. I mean manipulation of reality to satisfy our inner psychology needs. Be bold. Take psychological risks.

As a teacher and healer, there is so much power and good in words of confidence and faith, coming from a calm, clear example of someone who is to be believed.

Miracles happen when people believe in themselves. Literally.

Travelers

Susan and Lisa, February, 1986

Santa Cruz, California

February 9

Magic is alive.

Susan gave me longing looks and hellos at the Staff of Life. And said to me, "you look so good." Now I'm with her and Lisa at Seabright Beach. It feels good to live.

February 10

It would be so easy to lose the faith but I'm keeping my confidence up. This experience reeks of fate and a common destiny. But I still feature the idea that she is one of many special people I could meet. And I choose to bring it alive. To do; to act.

Although, curiously, so far, the patterns remain, of separation as soon as it begins.

Yesterday, at the Staff of Life, as I walked in, a woman smiled at me. And said hi and watched me. I knew I needed to take affirmative action. I shopped fast and got in line behind her. I hurried out as soon as I had paid. Outside she asked me for a ride to the beach. I said yes, this happening as she and Lisa were already halfway squeezed into the back seat of another car; with someone else who had offered to give them a ride. There was such a pull between us but they were like too committed to the other ride. She said "You look so good." I asked where they were going. She said Seabright Beach. I did a quick errand first, then went to Seabright Beach and found them quickly, scanning the beach from the cliffs with my binoculars. She was looking up, like she knew I was there, and saw me.

The rest is history.

She (Susan) and Lisa are traveling.

Susan is confused about a major decision. Where to go next. Maybe Hawaii. Maybe Harbin Hot Springs. But probably Florida to take care of her suddenly single Grandmother.

The three of us stayed at the beach a while, learning to appreciate each other. It was so much us all together; this time was meant to be for us for each other. There was no doubting the magic.

Fred was missing though. I knew he would complete us. And I wanted to share them with him and him with them. I called him and he was home and free. And I sensed he knew how right it was to join us.

They had no plans and let me lead. We made one errand stop for them, then on to Fred's house to pick up Fred, to Rodeo Gulch Road ridge for sunset, and Govinda's for dinner. All the time in the car we listened to, sang to, shared, and absorbed music. They were loving it. So were Fred and I. I drove the whole way down from the ridge at just a few peaceful miles per hour while Crown of Creation played and we sang and the little cubicle that was the inside of my Volkswagen bug was filled with love.

There was an endless stream of hand holding and gentle affection all with each other. They are lovers. With each other. And it seemed like near the end of the evening, Lisa, sitting in the back with Fred, really let go to the feeling of being turned on by a man, and that Susan was uncomfortable. She felt less with me than she had been. "And though my life was filled with wonder, my heart still knew some fear." I got into my head about them leaving and about not getting more intimate with Susan, taking me also out of the moment.

Still, it was altogether one of the most loving, completely Free experiences I've had. We/I could all be completely ourselves/myself and were totally appreciated.

At 10:30 Fred and I took them back to near the freeway to their "home." To their pine tree where they are camped. We had offered them to stay with us but they wanted to stay where they were camped. They feel pretty certain they're going to Florida today. Hitch-hiking. They have Fred's and my phone numbers. And Fred's address. Susan says she doesn't write but she comes back.

Don't guess I'll wait, but...

They sure were special.

I feel I could, in a relationship, work with Susan. She has much integrity. Very much integrity.

Had I been alone, I think I would have cried a lot when they left us, drifting away from my car and into the night. It wasn't easy for any of us. As it was, I cried a bit, and Fred and I drove home. I felt and still do feel kind of stunned. And alternately I feel so much caring in my heart for them. And, I guess, lonesome also, wanting a woman who I feel I could grow side by side with.

Magical Connection

Genuine affection
Parallel direction
In between the lines
Why!?
Why try to be otherwise!!??

There was too much left unfinished that I felt I had to communicate, but that I felt last night it wasn't right to change the energy for. That was last night, but today I had to find them before they left.

I drove to and checked out by the freeway on Market Street where they had camped.

I drove to the Emeline entrance
drove to both Morrissey entrances
to Staff of Life
to Community Foods
cruised Water Street to Pergalisi's
checked inside Pergalisi's and out in front
cruised the Mall
headed for the Ocean Street entrance.

Then I found them across the street from Mary Ann's Ice Cream place.

Perspective. More love. Some resolution.

Susan brought up almost immediately that she was jealous of Fred. And that she felt dirty inside compared with Lisa's youthful freedom. (Susan is about my age; Lisa, much younger, is about Fred's age.) She said she was being not so nice to Lisa today. And it can never be the same now.

We talked much more. Sharing our hearts, our fears, beliefs, styles.

I feel it really helped. A little bit of an adjustment into friendship mode. Still poignant, but joyous also.

She is a little hardened from hurt from an all-timer love affair. She knows it. Still, she gave me much affection.

Lisa was quiet. Kind of hung there, listened while Susan and I talked, and let us struggle. Wonderful goodbye and hugs with them both. See you later said Susan. Sure!

Gracious Goodness.

February 11

Some notes on me.

I'm feeling so much the sense of four beautiful loving humans free on the planet. I was really turned on by all four of us having long hair. It felt so real, natural, and powerful. Banish any thoughts of a major cut. Up at the outcropping in Rodeo Gulch, in the sunsetting hues, I looked at Lisa, Susan, and Fred's and my silhouettes and long hair flowing and it was so beautiful.

I continue, amidst tiredness, and some sorrow, (Susan and Christine encounters turning me so on and coming so fast to pass) to be aware of what I must Do to keep my love alive and to make it happen.

It's raining out. It's warmer. I feel cozy. I feel at home; welcome and wanted here at Fred and Dave's. I'm in love with Fred madly. I feel warm, good, and a little sad thinking of, feeling in my heart, and seeing the images of Susan.

goodnight

All You Need Is . . . .

February 15

Susan. I don't think of her often but when I do, it runs deep. I'm still kind of stunned. I hope she writes. I miss her. Time? History? Who cares. I miss her. Society standards might suggest that we needed more time together and a history together to give validity to my missing her... tell that to my heart.

Observing myself, I'm happy with what I see.

I remember those days of exciting events I used to have. I'd get wired, stoked on life and events, and it would collapse.

Now I'm sustaining such deep love.

I've integrated easily stroking and showing my affection.

I'm writing letters.

I'm running without counting the miles or being hung on consistency or results.

I'm playing some flute.

I must also say I question what sort of physical services I might do with the ease I have.

I know I don't want schedule.

February 23

You know, I feel so unhappy.

Even Though

I feel less grudges than ever before.

I feel so little resentment.

I don't think I've ever felt so little competition.

I feel so forgiving.

I feel so appreciative of everyone's beauty.

I don't feel in any hurry to change anyone.

So why am I so unhappy?

(Little voice knows. Ya want the answer? Try putting "except with myself" at the end of each item in that list.)

The tension is gone. So much tension from dishonesty and envy and need. Could it be that now I must find something in love to raise, to refine. I just don't know.

Epilogue

Though I looked and kept an eye out for her for a long time, Susan never did come back.

The Xtabay

Eugenia, April, 1986

Prologue

On the back side of the cover of the album, Yma Sumac... Voice Of The Xtabay, an album of exotic and unusual music, it has the legend of "the Xtabay".

The Xtabay

(From An Ancient Legend)

The Xtabay is the most elusive of all women. You seek her in your flight of desire and think of her as beautiful as the morning sun touching the highest mountain peak. Her voice calls to you in every whisper of the wind. The lure of her unknown love becomes ever stronger, and a virgin who might have consumed your nights with tender caresses now seems less than the dry leaves of winter. For you follow the call of the Xtabay... though you walk alone through all your days

It seems to me that virgin in this could mean the innocent wifier or wifeable woman, less highly erotic or exotic than the Xtabay. And "in every whisper of the wind" is my night time dream world. Or my fantasy world. Yes, I do seem to be seeking ultimate magic in love of and with a powerful woman.

Santa Cruz, California

April 25

I'm on fire. And it's so deep inside.

Two nights ago I saw two movies with couples so equally in love. So much wanting to be by each other's side.

I'm just aching for a companion.

Sitting in my car in the Community Foods parking lot, listening to my tape player, Beethoven's String Quartet #14 was divine. I would have melted, except I'm so hard. Afraid to melt alone. No one to puddle with.

Patti, who I know, not well, and from I don't know where, said hello, how are you when we passed in the store. I wanted to take her home. I choked. She was so beautiful. Stable adult woman. Christ.

Then I passed a woman in a car who looked at me knowingly and waved, I felt I knew her but I don't know. She looked like Susan.

Amazing. It's been ten weeks since I spent the day with Susan and Lisa. Ten weeks. Ten weeks in this weird middle mood. A kind of easy cruising cover over the absolute anguish and destitution and aching loneliness I feel.

Plain and simply, I am not happy.

Driving in my car tonight tears caught up with me. (I guess I wasn't driving fast enough to keep ahead of them.) It goes on day after day, week after week.

All day I've been aching for femininity. Made only more painful by the knowledge that all that I am is of my own making.

I've avoided closeness all day; maintaining a shabby veneer over my waiting tears and pain.

Any argument for my pain falls apart knowing the truth that were I radiant I would take my body to where the environment enhances my powers and wherever I was I would infect people with life and be helped and be vitally alive as a part of their lives.

I feel like the Susan experience had really deep profound effects on me. No sooner had I decided to radiate and be in my power, than I meet an incredibly special woman, and it felt so much deeper than the theorized idea that in my confidence I can just create a bond. She's gone as soon as she's come.

And I doubt it all; I lose the faith. And I haven't believed enough since then to carry myself free.

I went to Allegra's party last night. Dorinda was there, walking in barefoot, looking magnificent. We danced for a while. Later she came and laid with me and asked me about if I ever think I just don't deserve a relationship, meaning she's in the same boat. And that it seems like a big cosmic joke. She wants to be in a relationship so much.

We cuddled and it felt wonderful to stroke her. I was frustrated and, I guess, mad. I was so willing and so loving, but she's said no so many times to me.

I left disgusted. I wanted to be sad and cry but I guess that's not what I really felt. I feel like giving her a real kick in the ass from a friend. It makes me sick. The White Knight syndrome. And she can't love a friend.

I'm so tired and I feel a lot of anger. For all the fucking games. "I'm getting tired of saying do you come here often." I'm sick of people's fear of being close.

I feel like I did years ago in Olympia and Seattle. Just asking. Do you want to play tennis, take a walk, talk? Do you want to make love? So much fear. It's just communication. The stakes are higher. That's it. Fear of losing. But the reality is there is nothing to lose. I think I really resented last night that I couldn't be honest with Dorinda. If I express myself she freaks. Old shit takes over.

April 26

Today, somehow, telling Ragini of my solitary life and her reaction has made me feel sensitive to it. Also, these days, having free time to feel. I was aching for woman all day today. I feel that although I feel straight, tall, and bright, these days, I am just too something or not enough something to want to be intimately loved by women. It just simply doesn't happen.

I am aware of tremendous tension in my body like snapping these pens in half, like smashing walls, like disintegrating a wooden chair. Reducing the integral design of things to parts. Denial of the significance of structure. Since it doesn't work for me, I'd be happier if it didn't work at all.

Some thread of civilness is holding me together. For better or worse - I don't know.

I ache with longing. I feel it in my arms.

April 28

I don't know if I can handle the pressure of my physical frustration. My whole core from my pelvis to my head rushes, shudders, and feels pressure; especially my heart.

Seeing a woman stroking her boyfriend was agonizing. Such an incredible feeling of emptiness; no, not emptiness, I'm full of plenty; just a void.

I'm seeing women and feel/remembering the energy I feel while loving touching and the bodies shimmer with openness.

I had forgotten. And now it's flooding back. And I see my level of caring about my diet disintegrate. I ate many sweets this weekend. It's like why should I care for this vehicle in which and through which I perceive so much frustration and displeasure.

It seems so absolutely hopeless.

I seem so absolutely helpless.

April 30

Driving to town today, as soon as I dropped down from my home in the mountains and into civilization, the insanity hit. I feel totally in despair. It's like every nerve in my body is screaming to run this love juice and express it physically. Having the love in my heart and mind isn't enough to just let go to and feel that it's sufficient.

May 4

Realization.

(As if I believe in them anymore.)

(But maybe I just have to.)

The Love and Sex Dance

Face it! I can't take rejection - but wait a minute, you say. This person has reached out to almost certain rejection situations many times before.

Still, the truth is - same old truth (sort of) - that I am; I must be a powerful part of a Brave New World.

Which means that I know I can love easily, comfortably, freely.

I really am capable of Free Love. Meaning sex and the whole thing.

I'm faced with an opportunity - a problem/possibility to bring my life; my personality up to my soul's desire or wallow in the anguish of a mediocre life.

It's that simple.

The question is -

Do I have the guts? ! !

Now that's spiritual.

May 10, Davis, California

(Attending the Whole Earth Faire)

I feel confused, cheated, and devastated. And somewhere deep inside, a little flicker of rightness and goodness and appreciation lives.

But mostly tears and anguish.

At the Faire today I met and played hacky-sack with Anne and Eugenia, among others. I enjoyed a long hug and caresses goodbye with Eugenia and we made vague evening plans.

I thought I'd never find her later, but I did, dancing. She was so glad. Me too. Then she took off to find her sister. The dancing ended and the evening pow-wow started. I gave up on her coming back. She hadn't returned and I started to head out, sad and lonely.

I decided to eat at a booth first, then tried one more time to tour the circle. I found her and again we were both so glad.

She is Greek and so sensuous. Amazingly beautiful, lush body and soft sincere honest eyes. We were both so affectionate. Walking, strolling, with my arm around her shoulder, she placed my hand on her breast.

I can't write anymore. Maybe tomorrow. Suffice to say we built a friendship - that's forever - and we shared pleasure of holding and caressing each other (she is so sensuous) - and that is gone. I want more.

I discovered how much I have forgotten that I can please a woman. That my touch and caress and nuzzling and kiss is desirable.

Just a taste.

I just can't have it. I can't and I don't know why!

I want to hold her, keep her warm, show her how not to be afraid, protect her, and make her laugh.

The pain is almost unbearable. Some moments, I really literally feel like I'm going to burst.

More sobbing. It doesn't make sense. An hour ago I was holding a warm female human to me, with open hearts and eyes. It's over!

May 11

Last night I had this dream. I was in Greece. I was in a room, set up with a young woman to have sex with. She didn't want it to be like that and was distant and cool. I showed her I cared and we became friends. We left the room together and we enjoyed each other.

The Love and Sex Dance

Later I was in another similar or the same room with another young Greek woman. At first we were exposed to the outside, but we closed the door. She was willing to be my lover. But I just had no interest in her. My heart was with the first woman.

It is late afternoon and I am writing from the middle of the quad at the Faire.

I feel obsessed. Obsessed with the desire to feel what I did last night. I didn't see Eugenia today until about 4:00. She's not being very affectionate today. It hurts. It's really all I wanted today. I really don't feel like I will ever enjoy myself again without being sexually satisfied.

I realized today how vulnerable I am. Yes, Eugenia is just as beautiful to me today. I remember the taste and smell of desire in her mouth. I have never before tasted and smelled sex in a woman's mouth as I did with her. That is a lot to let go of.

And I feel this desperateness and fear that I'll never again be close to another woman so juicy and sexually open. But I know she's not the only one. And truly, sometimes I feel I want to have sex with every woman I'm attracted to because they are all individuals and sex is such a medium for touch and playfulness and honest expression and sharing of the heart. I guess it's just been so long since I've felt that chemistry.

Evening now, home, back in Santa Cruz.

This afternoon Anne and Eugenia came to me, saying they were going to dinner. Because I might not see her again, I said a warm goodbye to Anne and then walked aways alone with Eugenia. She said she was a little nervous today but she was glad to see me again and appreciative of our friendship. I really appreciate how willing she is to believe in our friendship and appreciation of each other.

I feel so much love for her.

Touching with her feels so good.

I feel better now. A little hint of peacefulness in reaching out, being a little lucky and sharing love. And some strange combination of satisfaction and sorrow.

Listening to the Righteous Brothers on headphones, Soul and Inspiration, it's so rich. Awesome vocals. So rich in emotion and impact built in.

Ebb Tide - I can't believe what I feel and hear. Incredible words.

May 12

I've been touching and stroking my friends so easily today. Touching women's cheeks and kissing them. Truly Eugenia gave me more than I was aware of.

I still feel a deep sexual desire to make love. But sexuality with Eugenia was, I guess, a real validation that I have something worth giving.

The weekend at the Faire has really given rise to questions about my whole lifestyle. It's not just the pioneering spirit of traveling. I meet people; I am magic when I play. Eugenia commented on my eyes in the hacky-sack circle.

How can I expect to be attractive hanging out glum in a noisy cafe. Clothes don't make this man. Eyes and grace and smile make this man. And I gotta play.

The Love and Sex Dance

It makes no sense to work all day and seek socialness tired in the dark. I need, or I should say, I'll need to radically question work trips in my future.

Interestingly, I also had an opportunity to observe my pleasure in people balanced against my need for quiet and to be away from the action and all the energy.

I gained greatly this weekend from leaving the hubbub and changing pace. Truly I need to have quiet, solitary time in my life and I need to be playing in public. I thrive on the strokes, and the opportunity to turn people on.

Yes I am an artist.

So... it's late. Midnightish. Lights out in a moment.

One last thing.

For all of what I've just said, so much has come from allowing myself to receive validation because Eugenia was so naturally open with gladness for my appreciation of her. She validated my loving.

So I'll say it again. Thank you very much Eugenia.

May 16

The last few days I have often felt my heart so open. It's a rush, a wonderful high; I feel so vital and full of love to give. And it hurts.

Eugenia told me that she may be moving to Santa Cruz this summer to work. Today the ultimate irony of that struck me. Though we have hardly developed a relationship of sexual lovers, I have been so turned on and it crosses my mind to not go to Europe as planned. So often I have been wild and traveled to see or be with women. Now it seems just as crazy to consider staying to be near a woman.

I ache for the love and the chemistry I felt with Eugenia.

I also ache for my Austrian friends, Edi and the Kerbers and for travel and speaking German.

I am doing better than I have in 9 months and I'm devastatingly confused.

May 18

I feel confused about Eugenia. I think mostly that the feeling and memory has faded and that it hurts less but it's harder in a way because I'm trying to still feel it. Again it seems unreal to me that someone could enjoy or want me so much. But knowing that is a part of me.

Fantasies and desires to be bold and express my desire to physically love women I know in town - Dorinda, Maria, Jane Rose - are virtually gone. It feels like it couldn't be the same without them wanting to nuzzle and fondle and be like Eugenia was with me. Shades of my dream after the evening with Eugenia.

Last night Karl and I and Andy went to Govinda's. We were an intense emotional triad. Andy was so hurt. It is so hard for him. We went with him to offer support and shoulders to cry on when he went to see Marcie, working there tonight. It was kind of a hard way to first see her after she had told him her feelings were somewhere else, because she couldn't take much time. The first time they spoke, he said "it's good to see you", then "it hurts," and she just walked away. It really hurt him. Men are such emotional wimps. We three were wonderful together. Karl is having it hard too. Living with two ex-lovers who he cares for so much. And Marisa and Bart being lovers.

I felt glad for us all being so open and risking that kind of vulnerability.

The Love and Sex Dance

May 19

Yesterday morning Dorinda came over to go for a bike ride with me. I was still in bed. She sat on my bed and we talked. I asked her about her friend Wally and that I see her with men a lot that look like they've asked her out. She started talking about things - men, fears, chemistry, sharing more personal stuff with me than she usually does. I told her about how I had been mad at her. We touched and hugged and as it would fall, we made love. After two years of knowing each other. I enjoyed it, though that was yesterday and I am now reflective of why it doesn't seem all that exciting to me.

I have this feeling that had I made love with Dorinda before I met Eugenia, it would have been more exciting and satisfying. (Eugenia is the Xtabay? My male version of the White Knight syndrome?)

Dorinda seemed, once she let us become sexual, very hungry to give love with her lips and hands. And also very hungry to have a man inside her.

At times warm tears filled her eyes. I asked her if she was ok and she said yes, it was just so much feeling. She said she felt a rush of energy from me. We were very affectionate.

Later -

I just talked on the phone for a half hour with Eugenia. Oh my God. Her openness and lush vitality and tenderness are too much. My heart aches. She is so sweet. Have I ever known any woman that I felt so mushy about.

I felt and feel so much love and affection in my heart for her.

I did learn that seeing her again before I go to Europe or staying because of her possible move to Santa Cruz are not what's to be. She just melts with appreciation for my desires for her, in her saying "no" to my suggestions. God she's special.

So there you have it.

Driving up to Fred's, Bach's Toccata and Fugue in D Minor was rushes from my oh so open heart.

I feel so strong and healthy and vital. And I feel some anguish. Joyous anguish.

In physical presence in my life, Eugenia is history. It's so hard being a traveler. So much to let go of.

I listened to Ebb Tide again at Fred's. Incredible rushes of emotion from my open heart, tingling out through my body.

May 20

I'm tired. Five and six hour nights of sleep the last two nights. I feel a little drained from how incredibly open my heart was last night. I keep having memories of Eugenia's voice and words. She turns me on incredibly. I told her that I felt she was going to have a good life. She cooed "Do you know how good that makes me feel." Oh my god...

May 21

My heart is so open.

Music, my God, music!

It was an intense day today. I feel unstable and kind of lonely, really lonely. Like the kind where I know that no matter how much love I share in my life, no matter how many loving friends I have, I have to overcome my emotions, my physical imperfections, my problems, and no one else can decide for me.

92   May 28

Dorinda was helpful, patient, and radiant today. She really turned me on. I asked her about our making love. She talked about how the strong romantic aspect wasn't there, but how good she felt about our love and affection and letting herself love just for what it is. And our honesty. I feel really good about having helped show her how we can be for each other.

The other day I was thinking how we live, we take it in, we take it on, and we thrive or retreat, but we always bounce back. We have rubber souls. Oh, my God! The Beatles! 21 years ago they saw it. We have Rubber Souls.

Open Honest Love

Monika, July, 1985, June, 1986

Imst, Austria, the night before I'm off to travel,
hitch-hike north to Copenhagen.

July 14, 1985

I really felt glimmers of knowingness with Klemens today. We share a deep bond. He asked me about major changes in my life. I gave him a brief synopsis. A blend of studious and wild, exploring teenage emotions with Kevin, psychedelic drugs, 20's search for the one and only, metaphysical rebirth.

He told me that that's just about how he thought it would be.

He said he'd really like to know my friends. And wishes he was born twenty years earlier. He's a hippie dreamer. But he is in the right place at the right time.

We went to visit his friend Maria and her friend Claudia was also there. We all hung out in the warm evening air on a mattress on the deck above their beautiful back yard. Soon he and Maria were touching and I was touching Claudia.

I felt very easy and the chemistry felt very right for me to be intimate with Claudia. She seeks to be such a free, true spirit. And has a wonderful touch. She has a tough home life, but high ideals. She said she wanted to be honest and told me that from the first time she saw me, there was something she didn't like. She didn't know what it was but didn't feel it to kiss me, though touching was nice.

Following certain things I said, a few times she kissed me tenderly, or hugged me tight, showing how much love we shared. I felt a little sad for a few minutes but that dissipated. I left feeling absolutely nothing but good about it all.

Not even guilt about touching such a young woman intimately. Too much love. Too much to have doubts, that is. A psychic flood of fresh water over the netherlands of doubt and fear.

Later, Klemens and I talked; shared about women and loving. A really nice personal sharing with my new friend.

Oh my.

July 15

Now in Karlsrühe. (Germany)

I'm on the roadside. I must write now.

It totally blows me away. But that's ok. It's my natural state. I almost can't control my laughter.

So much love with Bernie, who just gave me a ride, and his two friends. It's 7 o'clock. He gave me two numbers and told me if I don't get a ride I...

Now, it's an hour later and I'm in Frankfurt and two rides down the road.

Finishing the sentence above that was interrupted by rides ...can stay with them tonight.

Monika and Jo picked me up almost immediately after I got out of the first ride. Beautiful inspired women. Living communally. (That seems to be more special in Europe; less common than back home.) When they asked about differences between home and here I had to go a little into speaking English and give them an optimystic rap. They are into their own spiritual Reichian blend of loving discovery. Wow. They welcomed me to visit them.

Goodbye and hugs. Monika was/is incredibly attractive to me. I will return.

Witnau, near Freiburg, Germany.

One year later. Traveling Europe again,

staying with a couple I met, Sissi and Fritz.

June 2, 1986

I've been wondering a lot about my desire to visit Monika.

I wonder how much she remembers me, having spent only a very short time together, in the car with her and Jo last summer. I'm drawn by how attractive she was to me. And that my impression of her reminds me so much of Susan. Who is gone.

I wonder how crazy it is wanting to see Monika. Driven by heart and glands.

July 9

I'm flying through reading The Mists of Avalon. Was it pure chance or some sub- or semi-conscious thing that I started reading it on the Solstice?

I'm very involved in it and curious. But it's weird. With the exception of Taliesin and maybe Arthur, everyone is lies, cheats, and deceptions. Strange, it features the women's thoughts and power. Yet not a one is honest to her heart or her true wisdom. Every last one is pitifully ruled by guilt or driven by a means to an end. Weird.

After 200 pages of darkness, Morgaine now knows she deserves all she is; knows she is needed in her power; knows she is goddess. Just as I felt the next 300 pages would just be playing it out, there's light.

Will it take me 200 pages? God. I feel I'm in some dream. Where is the child's joy in summer fruit?

I've really got to be around powerful people or alone or move.

I had thought to maybe visit Monika as I went north to Denmark and Norway. Now I would like to just blast up to Karlsrühe, where Monika lives, and say hello; resolve my questions. Fuck the guilt. If I only want to go there because she turned me on and because Susan reminded me of her - that's enough. Enough?! That's everything.

Lay down beside me. Love ain't for keeping.

I wonder how Claudia is. (*different Claudia; German friend Claudia - not Imst Claudia) I wish I could just shower her with power, take her into the forest to hunt and forage and make love in flowers - with flowers! It's a great feeling to want to give that to her.

But, alas. It's so seldom we lay our Karma so easily aside.

Who among you will run with me?

The Song is Over.

I'm left with only tears,

I must remember.

Even if it takes a million years.

Seems like I must be near the end of those million years. Once there was a way to get back home. I can smell it. But there is so much mist.

I know it!

God, if I could only feel it!   If I could only feel it!

July 10

I just had an emotional talk with Sissi. She was defending Claudia as being cautious, not afraid, because of the way men are. I'm pissed. Sissi's afraid of touch. It's so simple.

Yesterday I, watching people in the city, was overwhelmed, with what a shame it is that cities aren't great meeting places of souls; of people sharing and trying to unravel the mysteries and being vulnerable and admitting our neediness, instead of rats racing to work and errands and investing in the future.

I read Jim Morrison's eyes last night. Yes we can look, but we cannot touch. Is it because we don't believe we can handle it? Is touch plain and simply the focal point, the most magnificent trial on this plane?

I'm pissed and discouraged. And though my self value is low right now, still I know I should never compromise my desires. Never. The only fault in our (in my) desires is guilt. Because we don't think we're good enough to give it back, we don't want to chance receiving it. - Oh, are you needy? Hey, not me. You got a problem. What?!! (shock) You admit you're needy?! My responsibility then is too great. You're like all the others. Take a hike, pal.

Christianity thrives on the same principal. Simple. Since I'm so incapable of loving; since I am "only human" and pitiful, I know I can do no miracles. All forms of magic and genius must be invalidated, so our idol remains intact and so there is and has been only One person ever who is capable of these things.

The Love and Sex Dance

Boldness, psychological risk taking, belief that we are capable of changing our own lives, and ultimately belief that our hearts have the answer is bred out of us; trained away.

Strange Days, indeed.

July 11

Oh my God. After leaving a message earlier I just called again and got a hold of Monika. She was so unbelievably excited that I'm coming to visit. She was out a while this morning and worried she'd miss my call. What a turn on. I must have made an impression. I'm going up Sunday.

July 14,1986

It's just like we're sister brother lovers. We touch all the time. She holds my hand. She has no fear of communication. Be it touch or otherwise. We are so affectionate together. When we lie together and I try and draw back a little, because I can hardly handle it, she draws me in. She squirms with delight. And I too. We both feel we've know each other for ever. Or never. She just is. We just are. I could look in her face forever. And she says she could look in my eyes forever. She's a little surprised. I'm not, except at how she lets herself into this intimacy while she has another lover. It's so pure. She reminds me of Marilyn Monroe. A divine innocence. Her hopes and dreams and always the smile. She leans, she nuzzles. And I too. And she softly welcomes me.

I know (?) I'll never walk but a stretch or a few by Monika's side, but now - here - she is a mate.

She has a beautiful voice.

July 15

Last night Ralf, her boyfriend, and Monika and I went out to a friend of theirs for dinner. Back home, Ralf said goodnight to me. Monika went and kissed him, said goodnight, came into my room and said, "maybe we need an alarm clock." We.

So there I was sleeping with this soulmate lover, while her four year boyfriend slept in the next room. So pure. So easy. Looking in my eyes, she said again, this morning, "I've known you so long."

I have never felt so unafraid of the end that will soon come. I know it's temporary. I suspect I'll miss this oh, so compatible love by my side. But... the knowing. And such a validation. Of my knowing last summer, when we first met. Of what I believed in contrast to Sissi's inhibited fear - excuse me, "caution," and Claudia's fear.

Later -

It's incredibly late again. I'm sleeping alone tonight. I've been crying a couple of hours.

How can there be so much to pay for mistakes in the past?

How?

The Dream is Over.

Camelot - was it really ever?

Monika -

I've been kind of tired all day.

I finished The Mists of Avalon, except the Epilogue, this morning, and that I finished this afternoon. Oh God, I guess there's progress. I guess nothing's for nothing. Even if it's all wrong. How many times can we make the same mistake before we learn?

It's sad and kind of strange that for me this book just passed, in the end almost meaninglessly. Possibilities, opportunities, events come and go, just like its story. 25 days of reading.

Monika urged me to go with her to her aunt's for lunch, urged me to go swimming, urged me to go to the movies. Lying naked together in the sun was divine. She just holds me, and wants me, and pulls me to her, and holds me; really holds me. Her aunt is wonderful. The movie was totally inane. Stupid dishonest archaic problems.

Tonight, while crying or writing, I've listened to Druid chants, Music for Airports, Elton John, Ebb Tide, and Fantasy on a Theme of Thomas Tallis. So smooth, rich, and harmonious.

I love her very much. Very much. After midnight, she and I and Ralf drank champagne and she opened the birthday presents he had given her. I really like him. He is light and laughs easily.

He went to bed and she said goodnight to me, she would sleep with him. She said she would like to have us on each side. She left my room, and the completely unexpected tears just flowed. I think maybe the hardest I've cried since Lene. I've been long overdue this trip.

July 16
Happy Birthday Monika.

It's evening and I'm at a wonderful party in Monika's parents' beautiful garden. I had my opinions about -

(Wow - I just got an incredible hug and a kiss on the cheek from a woman whose name I don't even know. But I sensed since she arrived that she liked me, an attraction I felt too. She and her boyfriend are here from München.)

- how I've seen less affection in Europe. Well, this oughta teach me. All of these people are very affectionate. Men and men hanging out together. Kissing each other on the mouth goodbye.

I got an incredible, undeniable hug from Ralf. I really like him. I haven't really had much chance to get to know him on a deeper level. But I like what I see.

Monika and I earlier today -

I typed out Ebb Tide's lyrics for Monika, and wrote her something. Massage, melodies, and memories for her birthday. Then we listened to Ebb Tide together. She requested a repeat.

We kissed, gazed, hugged, held, and were basically enjoying ourselves. She really turns me on - opens my heart - when she squirms with delight.

A little later we found ourselves playing again. Her smile and eyes just melt me. She got really passionate. I asked her if she wanted to make love. She said yes. I want you inside.

I - we - really enjoyed ourselves. She is so sweet.

I really like Markus, Monika's brother. He's physically beautiful to me, too. Her mother is also very attractive. Nice temperament.

It was also nice at the party to see how beloved Monika is.

Good night!

July 17, back in Witnau.

This morning Monika and I slept in; hung out in bed. Monika and I took turns helping each other orgasm. I was really enjoying kissing her and her pleasure. Incredibly.

I was thinking afterwards of my personal desire, and maybe guilt; and that I need to stay with the feeling of the sexual exchange, the giving. Hey, it's like with food. That occurred to satisfy a physical hunger. It was pleasurable. Now, here I am. Satisfied and hoping to be as loving as I can. And thankful that a desire has been fulfilled.

So here I am back at Sissi's apartment, and Monika is on a train to Dresden. I found some nice words and shared some nice and warm touch to try and express my feelings for and to Ralf, upon our parting. Monika walked me to the freeway. It was a nice walk and, well, I guess, as nice a parting as we could have. She gave me a shell necklace.

As we are both alone and on the road, I suppose we think of each other.

I know I just have to keep pumping up my appreciation level, as, or if, I grow lonely.

The string of honest, straightforward women I've been touching grows. And I think Monika's maybe the simplest relationship I've ever had. She is incredibly pure and loving.

I could look in her face, in her eyes for ever. There's just no resistance.

So far, I'm doing ok. Maybe it's just so right, I'll just carry the love and take care of myself. Maybe I cried already enough two nights ago.

- - -

July 19, hitching south out of Freiburg.

I was feeling very lonely. Thinking I should just bail out. I looked at the sign post next to me and some graffiti said... "will nach Kalifornien." ("I want to go to California.")

I couldn't hold my thumb out. I don't want to try. I just want to be. I'm so lonely. Had I been almost anywhere else, I would have cried. I started to several times.

I was confused. No energy to hitch, but Bob's company in Luzerne is probably my best bet.

Maybe I'm just suppressing my feelings about Monika 'cause I just don't know how to digest it. Maybe it has something to do with the fact that I can't even really have fantasies; she and Ralf are and should be.

Is travel just a distillation of the Life-Death process?

When you have loosened the winds
You must abide by their blowing.

Going for the Heart

Anke, July, 1987

Santa Cruz, California

July 17

I'm wired on ice cream and chocolate... and I'm feeling generally incredibly frustrated that this planet isn't paradise.

I was surprised to find, today, myself insanely frustrated sexually. The energy was in my chest and a little in the solar plexus. Aching to commune. I really don't want to blame the world instead of myself - I am pitiful - but still... I don't fit in. We run around 75% business and 20% play (within limits) and 5% (or less) guts, admitting what we want... and even less believing (of course we believe - we just suppress it so we don't have to respond to it) that anyone else cares about these things.

I'm really torn about going to Harbin Hot Springs, but it would be crazy not to. I've been 95% business lately and I freak to think I can't handle being real for a few days.

July 19

Karin and I went to Esalen today; to their weekly market, to show my massage tables. I sold no tables and had virtually no bites. I was sexually frustrated and feeling pretty much like my massage table business is dead.

Van and Light were there, at Esalen. Light hugged me long and close. I had resistance. Its impact on my loneliness was too intense. Karin loved his hug, but before we left she hugged him again and it brought her frustration out too.

I watched some lovers for a while and had some deep feelings regarding how desirable it is for everyone. All the way home Karin and I had a big discussion about going for it. She supported me in not being intimidated by people who respond as if I'm a weirdo. I'm an incredible powerful sensitive man, very desirable and my intentions are hole.

In the evening I went to have dinner with Jane, who I met the other day. She returned a call of mine yesterday and we made a dinner date for tonight. Time to test myself out. I felt really included by her roommates. Three women. All teachers. Lots of talking and joking. I found myself commenting on things real to my heart. And they appreciated it. Anne went to bed first. She is also very attractive to me. Julie said goodnight to us and we hugged a long close hug and she said, come back. It felt really good. Jane and I talked and hugged a lot. She sensed my desire and told me that other menness around her had her in retreat right now. It was very hard for her to say but I told her talking about real things was what I care most about. We hugged a lot. When we parted I held her butt and pulled her to me. We held each other a long time like that.

July 20

This morning I had a number of sexual dreams I don't remember but I awoke after a special one. A woman, who it seemed I sort of knew, and I were walking converging directions across an open field. When we met I said, "how are you?" She said, "lonely," then turning to me, "men." And she melted the length of her body into a hug with me. It was euphoria as we held each other.

I ran into Mary at The Staff of Life today and when she gave me the little social teases about how she was doing I went for the heart. It felt good to approach reality. We hugged and I held her.

The essence of the day was that I shone brilliantly and I touched and I considered myself as a good find and all women as potential lovers. It was fine but I found that I was only the more frustrated for it.

Saturday was the day Pluto finally ended its last retrograde to within 6° of my moon. Perhaps that plays a role in my shift. A kind of release and whip forward.

The feeling I have is a little like being on thin ice. Trusting that this is me. And wanting to stay with it.

July 21

I felt pretty low most of the day. Kind of listless. I think it was being one day away from the validation of my experience with Jane, realizing I'm still single, and that feeling of thin ice; can I sustain my confidence. Same old lesson. That's all it is.

Karin and I went back and forth and back and forth and finally decided to come to Harbin, which is where I am now.

July 22

This morning, I awoke incredibly frustrated physically. One beautiful woman I saw was just too much. I must release those pent up aching rivers. Karin and I are both flipping out sexually. Strange world. I've kind of decided to reach out and ask for it, but it still doesn't come easy, as people steer away from the heart.

July 23

I've just spent the last hour or so lying with Anke. Earlier, together in the hot tub was bliss. She touches and kisses an incredible range from soft to passionate. And we always seem to allow it all to be right when it is.

Yesterday, after being dealt a minor set-back emotionally - Susan said we could go for a walk but never really got back to me - I saw Anke sitting on a bench at a lookout and swooped friendlyly in on her. I found it so easy to touch her.

We hung out at the lookout for hours. Very close and beautiful. She said she felt a limit to how close she could be with a man right now. Later she explained that she's received so much hungry vibes from men since day 1 here.

In loving reality and with always open-hearted stroking I said, well if you had a lover the rest would leave you alone. We talked about this place being a time for her to retreat. She asked me about Karin, thinking I was just running around. I explained how she is my closest friend, soul-mate, and sister... and not lover.

So we slipped up into the library and after hours of freezing awkwardness sitting outside, we eventually made love there, warm and on the carpet.

She feels so good to me.

Today I felt a little fear. Will it continue? Will she touch me back. Thinking how when going for the heart, the truism about seducing someone holds; if you seduce someone, you might get them, but you certainly can't expect them to stay.

At breakfast together, I sighed and she brought me out. I said I want our relationship to grow but not to intrude on her time.

She said she just comes from here (she put her hand to her solar plexus-heart area) and I said that's all I could ask for. And it's true.

We really enjoy each other.

July 24

Last night Anke and I slept together under my bag and on hers. This morning I awoke first and was reading when she awoke. She awoke and turned to me and said softly, "Ich liebe." ("I love.") I didn't really hear the "you." In my insecurity and longing for signs from her I wondered exactly what she said. Did she say, "I love you." to me?

It was wonderful lying together. I told her I wanted to go somewhere and make love. She agreed. After breakfast we went off for a lazy walk and found a marginal place in the woods, away from central Harbin. Flies, rough ground, ants.

But still it was nice. As we lay there I finally asked how old she is. I expected anything from 19-29. She is 31. It felt really like a relief.

I also asked about our future. Her story is that an on again-off again lover is driving a tour bus from San Francisco to New York next week. She's going to meet him and maybe go with him. She's not sure she wants to. She's not sure she can. I asked her to come to Santa Cruz in the mean time. I told her I want to continue to be with her.

She said no, but she couldn't say what tomorrow would bring. We really love each other, but...

She said we will just have to wait. She follows her heart, I think.

An old pattern appeared. I started thinking what a relief it was. Her leaving - our separating - would liberate me from dealing with the differences; with her ways that could be hard for me. It's easier to love the fantasy than the person.

But I overcame it nicely and loved being with her and being loving and teasing while we walked back.

July 25

So, the latest development is this. Yesterday, at 5:00, she took off with someone to go to Clear Lake. I didn't really ask who he was or what they planned to do there.

By 11:00 I still hadn't found her after checking a few spots. I was really missing her. So I went to bed alone, waiting for her to slip affectionately in beside me.

I awoke at 3:30 and she wasn't back. I felt really sad. She never did come. I felt hurt that it wasn't a priority and worried about her being ok. But also considering who knows what kind of circumstances might have arisen, knowing the loving she would greet me with.

In any case, I awoke time after time. I had many dreams about her and about people not coming and then finding out hurtful emotional stuff. Some really exotic dreams. But all disconcerting.

After I got up, I went straight to my car and listened to music. Time after Time. Beatles, Who's Next, and George Winston's December.

I haven't seen her yet today.

- - -

Later - Afternoon, now.

Well, it seems that my feelings and dreams didn't stem from just insecurity.

I just ran into Anke in the dressing room. Obvious resistance. It was the first time she didn't return affection, at least in her eyes. Not exactly true, but with reservation.

I said, "you didn't come back last night."

"That's just how it went."

"I missed you."

"I believe that."

"Why so much resistance."

"Because it's so."

She's going off to get a massage. I asked if we could talk afterwards. She said yes. And she kissed me.

I went into the bathroom and cried.

It really is my fate.

I am in agony of curiosity. It seems so unbelievable that she could have suddenly met someone else she wants enough more than me when there was so much love between us. But not to come home and to be so distant both.

For two days I had a woman, who I really wanted, who wanted me, who rushed back to me laughing for one more hug and to lick my face, before she could part.

And it's over. Just like that.

I'm going back to my car. I need to cry.

Why?

Why?

After her massage we met up and talked. Yes, she slept with another man. No, she didn't have sex with him. She doesn't want him more. She won't come with me to Santa Cruz. She won't sleep with me tonight. Probably with him. She wants to find herself. It's not all clear but I really love her and she loves me. I cried a lot and hard. She underestimates her loving. As we hugged bye for now, she said she may find that it won't go so well for her after I leave today. Heaven and Hell.

Home now. Back in Santa Cruz.

It all seems so bizarre. Really bizarre.

Before leaving, I went to Anke's tent to leave a love-note. She was there. It felt really fine to be in the tent after four days without feeling like I'd been in a private space. Homey.

We walked back from the camp area together and said our goodbyes.

We exchanged addresses. I gave her my picture and she really liked it.

I'm just stunned. And incredibly tired. Being away from her and there, the reality of our different styles struck me more. But, regardless of what may have come up, it was too much of a shock. I appreciate many, many, many, of her ways. She is very sincere and honest.

I loved being in love with her. Her distance today makes it harder already to remember the 40 hours or so that she gave me so much and was so playful, and rushing back to hug or kiss me once more before parting.

Strange life.

Strange life.

I'm just gonna get back in gear. Go straight for the heart. Visit Jane and her roommates. Love women.

July 26

7:45 A.M. Only six hours sleep. Maybe I'll still resleep. It's strange. Here I am, just back home alone. I'll always miss her kiss, nose rubbing, and touch. I'll forget it on one level but...

Last night before sleep I was thinking about her unhealthy habits and I felt it to share with her my concern coming from a real caring place. In my vision I felt highly capable and in my turf. Teaching her a little. Sharing what I know to be true. It is also a different feeling because at Harbin I was cautious, trying to win her, then to find a place to be lovers and asking for it.

Last night at Saturn Cafe, it was bizarre. Everyone seemed like machines somehow. It seemed like such a pitiful attempt to take a break. I felt tall and wild standing in the middle and thinking how perverted it seemed that I couldn't simply change clothes right there, if I felt it.

But for all of Harbin's specialness, I feel that for me it is also a little unreal. With Anke my health ideas and spiritual focus would have come in to play between us or with us. It's a powerful place, but for me, I think, it must be for short visits. I feel a need to play and work more. Were I to live there, which I have been considering, I feel certain that after some time I would want more from outside life. And need to do more than I perhaps could do there.

- - -

So I'm going to take Anke's loving as the strokes they were and as validation for my beauty and ability to be a desirable lover. There's no stopping me now. I'm going straight for the heart.

Bedtime. Or bagtime, rather. I'm going to sleep on the floor in my bag again. It felt good to be on the floor. After Harbin, sleeping on the floor feels right.

I went and visited Jane, Anna, and Julie tonight. I felt really disappointed in them. They just seemed young and somehow consciously avoiding their hearts. I don't think we should all be deep or serious all the time. But somehow it just felt shallow. They were nice. I like them.

Later, at home, some people came over to play Dictionary. We just finished and people are gone now. A deep loneliness and sense of loss crept in as I faded tonight. Really missing Anke. No pictures of perfection. I just wanted an outlet for that kind of intimacy and loving a little longer.

I just had a vision of what lovers do.

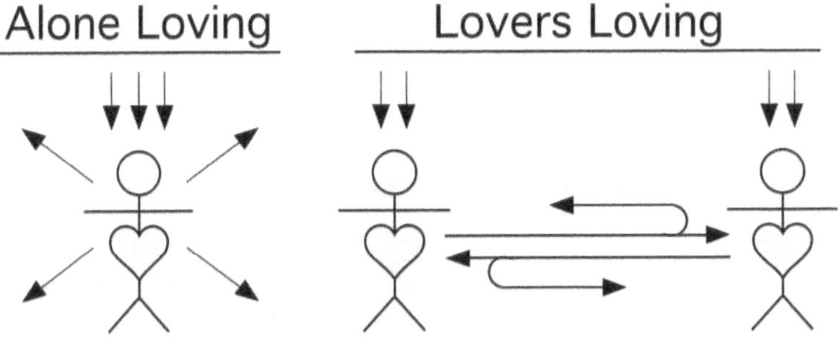

Love is transformed from undefined cosmic energy into human loving. Some love we hold for ourselves. Some love we give out. Alone we lose most of our outgoing love when we project it so much. And the only source we have is cosmic energy we transform. With a lover some of our outgoing love is taken by them and some is reflected in appreciation. And some of their outgoing love is taken directly in by us from them.

Lovers facilitate the movement and confidence incredibly. The love we hold for ourselves is necessary and good, but any that is pent up is stagnant. Energy needs to move. Knowing and feeling so directly that our outgoing love has value and is appreciated helps so much.

Visions Schmisions. I miss Anke. And it hurts a lot how fast she turned away from me. Strange patterns. Anke, Nancy, Lene. It's already been over as long as it lasted.

July 27

I just feel kind of stunned. The pictures remain. But the feeling is gone. I feel left with a bunch of puzzle pieces that don't connect. I remember moist electric sex and I remember being in my head and not very into it. I remember the incredible range of kisses and I hear her talking about being alone. I see her rushing to me and I see her rejecting my loving.

Both of each are real. I know that. But none of these seem real.

The week is here. She plans to leave Harbin today. Has she fallen in love with her other man in the last two days? Does she miss at all what we had?

I am a very, very lonely man.

Plain and simple.

Later -

One hour of work was almost impossible. Hard day. I feel really lonely.

I'm hurting so much from Anke and I know that through it I respect and love her and her honesty. I may not think her decisions are in the best interest of her heart, and I may not think how she treated me the best possible way, but I love her for honestly making mistakes, or whatever.

Later -

I feel I'm back.

It's good and I'm sorry.

I want - I really want to still feel Anke but it's passing. I'm just here in Santa Cruz, kind of lonely, checking out women. There is still a small hole, where Anke was.

I wrote her two letters today.

I still feel powerful and bold. I'm still going straight for the heart. Dan and Fred both gave me tactical information regarding how to deal with women in the last two days. But Karin affirms my style and I think it is where my power lies. Yes, I'd like a woman to stick around, but it's going to be because she knows she's getting pure and honest loving, and humor and strength and it's where she wants to be.

July 30

I have this emotional need / desire to know that all the love I was giving / trying to give to Anke was appreciated or meaningful. I think that's one thing hard about how she changed beds so fast. I felt that what I gave didn't mean that much; didn't make her feel all that special.

August 1

I ran into Alfredo from Argentina. He was with an incredibly beautiful woman and they were really enjoying each other. It hurt. I am really having to pull on my reserves not to be constantly in hurt mode. To recapture the spirit of boldness. To see the world as full of women who want to be touched by me.

I've got to go out and be alive with people. I can't calm down here. God, I feel desperately in need of perspective. I want to be the recipient of loving touches and kisses and ways, yes mostly the ways of a woman who turns me on as much as Anke did. I need to know she's not the only one.

Marijuana vision of my dilemma. My love is free and equal for all. I view all women as lovers, because to some extent I don't buy it that "one" woman is a need, to express my love to and be cared for. Conflict between my physical and ancestral roles to mate and pair off, and my planetary family consciousness of unlimited communication.

While listening to American Prayer I found myself reviewing my style. It seems I need to be alone with a woman and we need to have nowhere to go. It's rare that I get close enough to a woman with other company is around.

August 2

Awakening again with the feeling that it is incomprehensible, that it short circuits my reality to think I won't have sex today.

It is my life struggle. It seems such a waste. Were it like sleep; something daily that came naturally and satisfied my body and heart, and soul, I could live how I want.

I am so far removed from a natural, organic social life, that I spend no evenings just hanging at home, being peaceful - relaxing and expanding.

You know that feeling when you wake up from a nightmare in which something that was good in your life is gone. An emptiness. Cold sweat.

Today I awoke to a reality that felt that way. Daily life physical reality is the nightmare to me; the dream that I feel must be a part of my life, is gone. Even though I haven't had it for years it is natural and there is a void in my being for lack of a mate or sexual companion of duration.

August 3

I can't remember when I last ached so much for the loving of a woman, as I experienced with Anke, and feel also that sex is hardly alone my goal.

Today my sexual desire in public was beyond description and there were a hundred women I would have been glad to press my body against. Right now and the last hour or two, I feel more sexual pressure than I think ever before.

I briefly talked with Sean at the Credit Union after standing behind her for five minutes. Really a beautiful woman. I ached to press my body to hers and have both of us find pleasure in squeezing and stroking each other. I told myself that as she passed me on the way out I'd ask her to wait a second and try and get to know her. She passed and said goodbye and I chickened out. I have hated, hated, hated myself since then. I feel like I'll explode. And I'm filled with hate for myself and I have no faith in anything in my personal life.

Phantasizing sex. Hunger. I know that what I feel is a signal from Nature to get myself in order. And I am radically out or order. I am riddled with fear and apprehension.

I am a beautiful, healthy, vibrant man who handles himself so poorly so as to inhibit his chances. I make an incredible series of wrong decisions, almost unceasingly.

I feel like what has happened to some extent is that several months of intense work had pulled me far from my soul and heart's needs and desires. Now I have time and I have never ached more for a lover.

Phantasizing images of naked women, luscious open images of women did nothing until I imagined pulling their hips to me and Anke's hands over both of my ears and kissing me insanely hard and fast and deep as I moved quickly in and out of her.

God, I'm going to freak if I don't have a wild passionate lover again soon. Tonight.

August 4

11th day without making love.

It's just been hard to get back to post Esalen openness since Anke. I'm still subject to my psychology and it really devastates me. I was telling Karin about Sean in the bank and how I just wanted to touch her and effuse compliments for her beauty. Karin says think of it as a revolution that must happen. Be that vanguard.

Medilogue - During the next couple of weeks, as the great cosmic event, the Harmonic Convergence of August 17th, approached, my whole being shifted. I relaxed and the last few days before the 17th, I began to eat very little and sleep lightly and little. This occurred naturally, without my intending it. I wrote once, "I'm being compelled into a state of lightness."

After the Harmonic Convergence itself, my focus became profoundly cosmic and global. Tuggings of the heart were gentler and less personal. In early September I wrote, "Everything feels so different since the Harmonic Convergence. A lot of stuff is bubbling but it seems that dealing with it is softer."

And it was time to go to Harbin again. Of course, Anke was still on my mind and in my heart.

September 13

I think I'll go to Harbin Tuesday.

I feel that Anke has played very deeply in my psychology lately.

I wonder if I'll find myself hurt at her being loving with her lover, or hurt at them being so normal, or whatever.

I keep getting these feelings of deep heart love and affection for her. I suspect that what she says is partially true. That she just happened to be the one there. But I don't think it's that simple. She is honest, solid, sincere and the best kisser - the most compatible kisser I can remember. To experience the range from passion to tender matching my style and preferences or striking my chords so, is exceptional. And means as much to me as any sign or any feeling could.

On the other hand, maybe I'll be at peace, accept it, or whatever, and build a good friendship with her. I know she respects me.

Though I still physically ache for a lover and want a mate, I have had virtually no frustration or pressure caused or brought out by women in public since the Harmonic Convergence.

September 15

I'm at Harbin.

I saw Anke immediately. She is reflective. Her boyfriend on the bus tour abused her; hit her. She has fear of men; of being out in public. I know now without question that she was wrong. I don't just need someone and she was there. I love her. I care for her very much. She is very special to me. I love stroking her and loving her.

September 16

Funny how I feel about Anke. It's so light. There's wouldn't-it-be-nice-if-ness. But I don't feel hurt. I feel sad a little, but it's softer. I realized, today, that we haven't hugged; haven't held each other yet.

September 17

I saw Anke walking today and stopped her. I said, you know what, we haven't even hugged yet, and went to hug her and she threw up a wall and said no, she couldn't hug anyone now. She said it was in general and not because of me. I told her it hurt me that she had so much fear. I told her she was wrong before and that I indeed did and do care for her.

I asked her if we could go walking sometime. She said she isn't going anywhere.

It was extremely awkward. She has so much fear.

I stroked her a little and touched her innocently and she recoiled noticeably.

I now feel no longing for sexuality or intimacy with her. Instead I feel sad and a deep caring for her. I also feel rage against the slob that hurt her.

It's so strange how healing touch is and how that is just what she is afraid of.

September 18

It took me a long time to fall asleep. I kept thinking about Anke. I was thinking last night that I'm afraid of a lot of things, but at least not people, then I thought, yes I am. But I retain the belief in my ability to tell the difference. It must be terrible to have lost the confidence to differentiate between gentle people and dangerous people.

So, the last couple days I've kind of put it out that I want a woman who is healthy, trim, natural, intelligent, emotionally capable, and passionate, who will recognize the good in me regardless of my mood. And I won't need to chase her. I can't. I just can't. Somewhere out there is a love who won't run because I'm acting too low, too clinging, too crazy, too clean, or too dirty.

September 20

I picked a bouquet for Anke and found her at the lookout. She really liked the flowers. We had a nice slow talk.

I asked her to write and told her that if she ever needed a friend she could call. She said she'd be in touch.

I took her hand and she really held mine. Squeezed it and really touched me. It really moved me.

As we parted she thanked me for my friendship and hugged me. One hand holding the flowers but still the best hug I've gotten in a long time. She pressed her whole body to mine and was totally there.

It really turned me on. I really do love her.

Off now. Homeward bound.

I still feel deeply moved by Anke's reaching out today. It was like all of a sudden we were doing what we were supposed to be doing.

Her hand hold and hug were so strong and close. She is a very deep loving person.

Ok. I'm back.

Epilogue

In subsequent trips to Harbin I would see Anke and occasionally spend time with her. Our friendship was solid. She did indeed trust me and there was love. She still was somehow connected to her violent "boyfriend" and to her safe non-romantic Harbin "boyfriend." And she continued to be very protective of her space and cautious of men.

One day I found her in a small room doing craft work and came up to her from behind and touched her as I said hello. She jumped and the energy was intense. Fear. I spilled out an apology, saying I was sorry; I should have been more sensitive about how it is now for her with men. As fast as it had come, the fear left and the energy in the room was clean. As soon as she recognized it was me, she said, "Oh, it's you. That's different." Her eyes were bright and warm and her smile, ... the playful impish look I always loved.

Free to Love Again

Ancsa, Sheri, and Brigitte, August, 1989

Prologue

One and a half years had gone by since contact with Yolanda. I had not yet fully recovered; far and away the longest I have ever taken to recover from a relationship; to recover from far and away the longest I have ever allowed myself to be teased (by her and by myself). The most deeply my self esteem has ever been shattered.

It was a deep fall; a kind of quintessential disintegration, necessary for my soul to rebuild and purify my personality for the remainder of this sojourn. The work goes on.

In need of travel, I was heading north from my home in Los Osos, near San Luis Obispo, to Northern California, possibly Harbin Hot Springs, Chico, and maybe even up to Washington.

Los Osos, California

August 4

I just called Yolanda about visiting on my way through the Bay Area on my way north. Somehow our talk disturbed me. It seems like some combination of the awesome attraction and desirability coupled with realizing how her lifestyle - her style - could never have worked for me. I think it disturbed me because I feel I was had. And I'm disturbed with myself.

I feel a kind of a hollow space in my heart. I need a replacement. She still lingers.

The idea of a replacement person has always been something attractive to me while seeming also like a cheat. But looked at in terms of replacement love for the heart, it seems healthy and right.

August 5

I'm off on my travels northward. I feel hollow and desperate. I want to ask Yolanda to make love with me. Life is strange. I had a long, long talk with Karin last night. From a book of Austrian graffiti she gave me: "Be unrealistic. Ask for what you want." I don't know if I have the nerve.

August 6

Last night with Yolanda was perfect. We hung out, went out to eat, hung out some more, and talked.

I wanted to make love. She didn't. But we touched. Mostly I touched her and she took it in. She is absolutely one of the softest, silkiest women I've ever touched. She wouldn't kiss and wasn't into it with any intent but seemed to love being touched and stroked.

And... the phone rang, interrupting us, with one of her myriad arrangements with visiting or needy friends every time that she'd get really lost in sensation.

So all in all she seems to have been demystified. I love her sexuality. I adore her soft heart. And I have no illusions of ever wanting to deal with her harried life and her problems. And she really has problems. So many buttons.

I expressed to her at one point what I was feeling as I made peace with my feelings regarding her; that I didn't want her any more than I could have her. Beautiful.

I feel like after 16 months I'm free of Yolanda.

So I'm heading off to give Harbin one more try. I know I said I'd never go there single again. But I'm going to go and see if I can handle it. I feel freer and optimistic now. More so than I can remember feeling in years.

August 10
Harbin Hot Springs.
Amid total confusion as to where to next.

The Ancsa Story -
I approached her during a thunderstorm downpour on the main sunning deck. I was attracted to her and felt an immediate thrill from and affection for her. I wanted her.

I spent some time with her and got to know her a little. Night, I slept next to her on the sleeping deck. She let me know she needed space. She removed my hand gently from her body, but didn't let go. She held my hand a few moments more. What a beautiful softening of the space between us that she required. I was hurt and felt rejected, although I appreciated her communication and integrity. I cried. Strange sleep. Dreams. I felt again defeated but fought it, hung in there.

The next two days we palled around a lot. Yesterday, as I was about to go to Ashland, she invited me to go to the Tea

House and smoke grass with her. (*The Tea House is not a cafe, but a small one room building well up above the main area with a deck overlooking Harbin's valley.)

We spent a beautiful afternoon together.

She has a relationship situation that is complicated and she has critical choices to make. I felt so much in giving love to her and that it was the most important thing.

Today she called her boyfriend and asked him to come up here for her to share her decisions and contemplations with him.

I just saw them walking together. And this is why I wrote this little synopsis. I felt completely undisturbed by seeing them together and realized: I Don't Want Her Anymore Than I Can Have Her!

Now that for me is progress. As I realized and felt that, I felt yes, the Yolanda thing that had been living in me for so long is dead. And really Yolanda was only the extremist and latest. Maybe I am learning, or am finally realizing (meaning bringing into being) how I have wished I were.

August 11

Yesterday I immediately faced a challenge regarding what I had just written. Within seconds of writing, I ran into April from San Luis up here with her roommate Jennifer. I was humbled and it was ironic to be so far from conservative San Luis Obispo and meet two natural women with armpit hair from there. The challenge - Jennifer is as gorgeous to me as I can imagine a woman being. It was hard at first to not want her any more than I can have her.

August 23

I'm back in San Luis. I had tried to leave Harbin for further travels, but a strange car breakdown under the scorching California sun sent me back to Harbin, and I'd had enough adventuring for one trip. So I came home.

I went to a party tonight where I met Meegan. Incredible young woman. Stimulating and challenging. Intelligent and motivated. Also radiant and healthy and solid. I left her with my number and expect nothing, which is right. Interesting how, although she lingers on in me, I don't feel it to want what I can't have with her.

But I sure do want it with someone. Back home, I spent the evening in the now, feeling lonely and wanting sex, feeling kind of cheated, even as I'm aware that I am a new man and I'm being really different with women - at least with women who I'm reserved about or who I'd like to have.

August 24

I'm amazed still that I am alive again. And so much freer. The way I think of the women I meet is so much freer and I know I'm giving more. Meegan was really exciting to me but she's somewhere else until whenever she may enter my here again.

I called Juleen and asked her to go for a walk tomorrow. She's in finals. She's free after next Wednesday. She sounded sweet and like a friend. I want to love her madly but... hey... that's an adventure for me to play if she feels like participating.

September 5

Home again after a second trip up north to Harbin Hot Springs.

Stunned by the ultimate challenge thus far since the post Yolanda life, to not want more than what I can have and to believe this is a new life and put the old tape loops to rest.

For the blink in time that was called last night and this morning I had and was a lover.

Except that I knew from the start what the reality was that I needed to honor, I could have been in love for the first time in over a year and a half.

I met Dana and Sheri, sisters, on the deck.

We went on a walk to the Tea House.

I massaged Sheri's back a long time.

Wonderful, sane, playful women.

We walked down and all tubbed for two hours.

I massaged Dana for a long time in the water. Really soft and sensuous.

Dana drove to Sebastopol.

Sheri and I hiked up to sleep in the Tea House.

We sat outside on the deck in silence for a long time.

I felt so much loving and affection for her.

My arm around her waist, us looking out, she turned to me and softly said, "I want to make love with you, but I can't." She is coupled in a far away town, that is her home.

Without making love we drifted and surged and ebbed as lovers. Passion, tenderness, eye contact, and words woven so easily and gently together.

It was so hard to leave her today, but necessary. I cried immediately, then grimly drove home through major traffic. I have so much fear of my old loops. Aching, feelings of defeat, tragedy, and unfairness. She's already so distant. Part of me wants to hurt in anguish for how fast she's gone and how (in some ways) vague the feelings already are. But they're really not here. It's like in Golf in the Kingdom, having come into a higher state, observing the flotsam and jetsam of my romantic past, while I'm held in a field of positive vibrations.

September 6

So here I am back in the frigid foggy coastal weather. I feel really depressed right now. It just sort of descended on me since I've been home.

Right now I feel a real sense of loss, really lonely for and sad about Sheri.

Earlier today I felt tall and strong and felt happy just to have had a moment in time with Sheri, but now... it just hurts. I'm so sick of saying goodbye to women I feel I could share my life with. Maybe - probably - it's simpler than that. I guess it's pretty simple really. And it hurts.

Evening. I feel that kind of depression that I feel in the fall. Even with everyone around tonight, I felt and feel a kind of cold 2 dimensional emptiness.

September 7

We had to go to Santa Barbara for work today. I told Jim that I just needed to be alone, so I drove there and back alone in my car. I thought all the time about Sheri.

The idea that helped the most was simply that I could have cruised along in normal lonely seeking mode had we never kissed, and realizing what I would have missed, it seems worth it.

And I'm still dealing with the concept of her receding to a moment in my past, while I want to call her and hear her voice all the time and I want to see her again.

Later -

I just called Sheri. She says she's not good on the phone. She's trying to sort out what happened. It seems she feels she was unfair to me.

We talked long enough so she was able to say a few things that were expressed in the way she was with me when we were together.

Her boyfriend came on another phone and she wondered who it was and he didn't say and he hung up and she was really disturbed. I heard him in the background and she said, "It's a friend from California. Can't I talk on the phone?" or something like that. He yelled.

We spoke briefly after that but she was ultra-distracted. She had to go and deal with him. She asked me not to call again - at least for a while.

Just as well. I needed to check in once but I don't want to get into a phone relationship.

I feel now much love for her and sadness that another woman feels she needs to make it work with a man who feels he needs to control her.

I love Monika and Ralf so much for evidencing how I've always believed it could be.

Now my impression of Sheri's reality is changed. Sort of. I had kind of expected or felt it. Part of me wants to rip her away from him but I know that is really foolish. I expect nothing. I perceive she is deeply intertwined with this man and she is there and I am here.

I am somber now. In a way it feels simpler and I'm sadder now. I guess I'm feeling anger now and I want to defend her; save her from the dragon.

Talking, I felt it to continue an exchange of thoughts and feelings with her; for our friendship to grow, even if only pen pals.

I guess I'll have to wait for my disappointment and anger to subside. And wait for her letter. It could be a while. She has a lot to sort out, I guess.

One thing I know. I love her very much. ... Sigh. Sadness.

September 10

Sheri seems really distant. Make believe. I guess reality makes the past fade faster. I don't know. But I can't remember the feelings now. And the memories of what we did don't seem very important. It kind of disturbs me. It's almost worse than the hurting. And to get on with life; to be open to a new lover and mate and happiness while Sheri is just someone I knew once disturbs me.

My room seems like such a dead place. I keep wanting to get rid of all kinds of possessions but they're not the problem. It is the killing of time instead of the living I do here. Way too much TV. Isolation instead of time being alone for healthful reasons.

The first night at Harbin last trip I saw a shooting star and I wished for love and sex at Harbin. And I got my wish. I guess I should have asked for her to have a place for me in her life too.

I really miss Sheri. She has some amazing qualities. Her tenderness and a really special kind of grace and a quiet presence. Her integrity and sincerity and our physical compatibility make me feel I'd be willing to work hard to have a continuing relationship with her.

September 11

Trying to be philosophical, the only explanation, except that I simply have a lifetime of bizarre, hurtful, and rare relationships to play out, is that I am preparing myself (or being prepared) to be the most capable lover, friend, and mate imaginable.

Sounds nice, but I know just from reflecting on my desire to stay with Sheri that I would have to work (inner work) hard and hard for a long time to allow another person the space to grow and love freely with me in their life.

I am not complete. I am not very good at letting someone very different than me be the beautiful influence and teacher that they could.

September 13

I think I'm almost ready to let Sheri go and try and not want anything from her I can't have. I'm anxiously waiting for her letter to find out, I guess, what I can have. (Interesting concept - waiting to find out how much I need to let go of.) I hope as I try and move on physically we can write and be confidants and share ideals and visions, and love and honesty.

I feel better somehow about Sheri tonight. Somehow I am myself, which is what I came home with and I gotta go from here.

I've got to start flirting and being outgoing and playful again. I asked the woman, Leslie, at Phoenix her name today and saying something silly and nice as I walked away, still looking at her, I ran into a woman coming in. She was smiling and Leslie was too. Classic - man looking at woman pays no attention to where he is going. (What a metaphor.)

September 14

Last night Karin talked about connecting with herself and we talked about how I haven't for a couple of years. Today I took my Britton, Bliss, and Holst tape and my Walkman into San Luis, where it was a beautiful fresh hot day, and went looking for a nature spot. First I went to Cuesta Park and played some good frizbee with a couple of young men. Then I went to the creek by the high school, parked my car and walked up aways to a nice spot. I set the volume so I could still hear nature around me. The sun was lowering through trees. Water skimmers doing ripple tank experiments. I felt very much appreciative for life - just because it is. I tried to disturb insects and the world of the creek valley as little as possible.

I thought warm thoughts of Sheri from time to time. I asked about life; how the earth and animals just do their thing.

When the batteries ran out I read a little Walt Whitman and some Hesse out loud. A wonderful retreat.

I have been feeling really beautiful lately. After the sauna tonight when I came into the kitchen with clean hair in my bath robe, Becky was oohing and aahing how beautiful I was.

My posture's good. My hair is healthier. My skin is even reasonably tanned and I feel really healthy. At the co-op yesterday I had a convo with a man and woman about bee pollen and as I walked off I heard her say to him, "He looks really healthy, doesn't he."

September 15

I think not having gotten a letter from Sheri is really affecting me. I really want to know how she is and get a little feeling for her since us. I think it will help me. It seems I'm forever trying to make peace with left over emotions from extremely short relationships by myself. And on top if it, none of my friends ever have seen me with these women. I'm so glad Karin, at least, got to meet Sheri.

1:00 A.M. Well, I don't rightly know how it happened but I just kind of hung out after eating granola and yogurt and rice dream and chocolate sauce listening to the radio playing symphonyesque classical music and I somehow drifted into a kind of serene place. I quickly wrote off a beautiful love note to Sheri, appreciation for just exactly what we were, out of time and the rest of the world. That felt good.

The music has been divine. I'm not paying any attention to it, but it is so clear. I guess maybe a part of me is paying attention to it but I'm not following it.

So... Sheri Dee, I love you dearly. Together we were so sweet and graceful.

September 16

I feel desperately cold and lonely again. Cold inside, I mean. Flat and loveless. I feel like I'm shut out of a world in motion; empty and apart. I feel locked into suffering. I can't imagine turning my time in this empty house and sitting alone on the sand into feeling good.

I want to be a lover. Active. Warm, soft, giving, touching. I want what I felt with Sheri and, to be honest, what I felt with Sheri and Dana.

I think I'll call Fred now.

Talking with Fred helped me immensely. Explaining to him the state I was in with Sheri validated the high mature spiritual loving it was, because he understood. He believes in me.

Nice when compared to normal like when I tell of my love adventure with Monika and Ralf people always say "weird." They project their own limits and insufficiencies on our experience. They can't believe it was high mature spiritual loving.

At one point, together in the Tea House, Sheri had said to me that at first she thought I was just one of those guys who just wanted to get laid. And told her I was... but with love. And I explained to her that my sexual desire compels me often to pursue, but sex for me must include my need to communicate, to care, to be loving, to be present, and to be committed to our feelings.

I need that. I want to live in a society surrounded by people who shine, want to love, want to touch, want to revel in the pleasure of mature spiritual loves. Unafraid. To delight in Truth at all costs. To do what you feel is right, no matter what the rules are and let society and physical events follow, not lead.

September 17

It's a beautiful warmish windy day out. I feel absolutely totally apathetic. I don't want to do anything. I went out for a run and quit as soon as I got to the bay. I just had no drive. I liked the weather but had no patience to hang out there.

Year after year goes by and nothing changes. I feel like I'm functioning at about 1% of my potential to give, to love, to heal, to educate, to share ideas, to touch the world.

It's like every time I get high on shining and giving and loving I have a new hurt to overcome. Seems like always a loss to deal with. I guess I shouldn't hurt for losing that which I never would have had, had I never been open enough to have loved like I did.

But it's just so hard for me to let go of individuals and in this body I ache for the continuation of company at such intimate levels.

Becky and Deanne both called me this morning expressing appreciation of me and sounding kind of down. I felt too low myself to let them know how I feel.

Again it's late and I'm still up. Cryinalittle and listening to the Jefferson Airplane.

I decided in anguish to just sit and try and be high; to let what's important speak to me. I've been feeling the old same inability to love everything and fully participate before a woman comes and stays and/or I recognize her.

I couldn't really get very meditative - (I know - I tried for 30 seconds) - but I saw one thing. It's wrong to wish for Sheri to leave her boyfriend and come running to me. It's physical weakness compromising my spiritual consciousness and I must rise up.

With her, I told her I couldn't be with someone without wishing for all people involved to work it out. I really meant it. But of course she was with me. It was so easy to be spiritual.

I've got to move on. (Which I guess to me means looking in physical now reality for another woman.) I guess I just can't imagine living my life without looking under every leaf for "her".

The hell of it is I don't want to invite people I meet to do some social diddling. I want to sauna. I want to massage. I want to run and play.

Oh, Walt. Would that I could run free and not be afraid of being called a fool.

September 18

I got a letter from Sheri today. She wants to end communication because it's too difficult for her. I'm sorry. But it's also not so hard to accept it because her letter just oozed with emotion and caring and loving and appreciation and well wishing. She has an incredible heart.

I wish I was so physically, romantically, and spiritually satisfied that the memories were nothing but sweet.

I wrote Sheri a phenomenal letter back. She didn't want me to write again but I just had to appeal to her to not feel guilty and to just Love, Love, Love. And to let her know she didn't hurt me. I wrote it all on Yellow Submarine stationary. Beautiful and high.

I found a book in the poetry section at Phoenix today by Leonard Nimoy called You and I. It seems like a beautiful romantic and spiritual story about the search for a soulmate and the learning to live together and keep love alive. So it seems.

- - -

I just re-read Sheri's letter one last time before bed. So much emotion. It really sounds like it is difficult for her because she loved what we were so much. I think part of her keeps telling her she wants us and that's hard. I feel loved because of how well she expressed her affection and also how sorry she was that she needed to make a separation. I know she's not denying her feelings and I know I will always be loved by her and that feels good. And I don't know if I've ever had a lover express herself so well to me, especially amidst such a difficult situation. It is a validation of me, of our love, and of her integrity.

September 20

The morning sun's just come over the ridge. I'm at Harbin again. I wondered about memories of Sheri and I here together disturbing me, but I've been here too many times and it took place in my heart and between us anyway.

So far, last night, I didn't feel lonely. Only kind of grim. Kind of mellow and looking for the right woman's face and only minimally interested in bodies.

I want to read You and I, Nimoy's book, while I'm here.

It's strange here, this late in the year. Very quiet. Much fewer people. And everything is wet. No dust. And the ground is soft. It rained almost three inches here. Also an incredibly heavy dew. Even the deck hadn't dried by last night. It's fall.

In light of what I read skimming through You and I, I was thinking about being in search mode for a woman and how I should could ought to fully accept and validate that in myself. Admit to not now being capable of a free unattached happy-go-lucky life. And raise the search to the highest spiritual Love Quest that I can.

Curious. I sure don't remember feeling so alone here, yet I feel less lonely than I've felt here in a long time. I hiked up to the Tea House. Scene of magic time with Ancsa, Dana and Sheri, and Sheri. This time alone.

September 21

I'm kind of bored and lonely today and want to go over to Sonoma County and check things out but I don't know where I'd stay. It confuses me. Like sometimes when you're on the road, you just want to go home, but the sand trap of Los Osos is not the home I want to go to. It's strange. I don't feel like I have a home.

Home is where the heart is and my heart is lost. The last home I had was with Sheri Dee. And right now I really can't imagine any place feeling like home.

September 23

Last night I was looking straight up at the Milky Way thinking of Sheri and my heart was feeling a little open and soft and I saw a shooting star.

I wanted to wish for a woman who wants me and is also searching and I got this clear warm vision of a woman with long dark hair finding me attractive and actively showing her interest and seeking a relationship with me. So much different than my me pursuing women fantasies.

I saw two more shooting stars in the next minute or so then two more in the next 10-15 minutes, before I crashed.

September 24

Yesterday, soaking in the warm pool, when I first saw Brigitte coming in down the stairs I was struck by deep set wide bright blue eyes, a strong face and a kind of heaviness.

She saw me and really looked at me. I felt it to just hug her, words unspoken. I knew it would be ok.

She came straight to me. We said hellos.

Talk, touch.

She cried when I held her.

She has been fighting cancer, treatments, related complications, and pain since 1974.

She's not gaunt or wasted. Incredible.

She floated me around a while.

Then I held and rocked her in the water a long time. Love. Gentle kisses.

She is married. Lives back East.

We went down to my car in the parking lot to listen to a tape. In my car we got very sexual. She knew exactly what she wanted ... and ... she was unsure. I was also divided.

In the evening we went up to the Tea House. Curious reprise. While walking up the trail through the woods in the dark, I was watching myself, as if from outside. Didn't this man just do this with another coupled woman 2 1/2 weeks ago, who he's still feeling so deeply for? It's so good, but is it all right? We did, in fact, make love. I felt bad afterwards. Tamed, I felt like I'd given in to a weakness and made an unnecessary difficulty in our, especially her life.

We talked and I felt better and more loving and giving.

And with her, but aside from her, I knew I need to look at my loving and mature it. I don't exactly know what that means.

When we came back down, in the dressing room with Joseph, she looked so beautiful and radiant. Just shining. Joseph saw it and felt it and I could see it in how he was with us. He was wonderful strokes and understanding. He was about to head out, leaving Harbin. He and I said our goodbyes. Hugs and he kissed me.

Brigitte and I sleeping together in my bag was so easy. Well... except I didn't want to sleep; her touch and presence were so silky tender and I wanted to stay awake and revel in that. Also, she needed to leave early in the morning, and I wanted to feel her as much as I could.

We slept three hours and up before dawn our goodbye was wonderful and pure.

I will share music, pictures, and words with her through the mail and love through the ether.

Brigitte is gone. I miss her touch and strokes already but so far (which isn't far) I feel so good. No real sadness. Sometimes when she became playful I wondered if I was too challenging and maybe insensitive dealing with her illness. She said no and said, as she left today, that she felt a great weight lifted.

It really moves me that I could be such a lover and healer.

She said over and over that I was beautiful. Nymph like.

Earlier, talking with Terése, she said I could have any woman I wanted.

As I look at my experience with Brigitte, I've come to feel like maybe for the first time in my life that I need to mature my physical loving in light of how desirable I am to so many.

Still, I am high on Brigitte's strokes. Just gotta love.

September 25

Sebastopol - a friend's house.

Putting out my stuff here and settling into my bag, I feel good, even being alone.

I felt drowsy and strange most of the day. Partially, maybe, because of unfinished and undealt with and maybe unrecognized emotional stuff related to Brigitte.

I feel almost guilty that I let go so easily. And I wonder why. She was magnificent. Her touch, her loving, and her appreciation were wonderful. Her body felt really nice. All of her. I think somehow - I guess anyway - that maybe her marriage stability and my not feeling I could deal too closely with her physical problems take away the phantasy element. I think it's important I keep these questions open. Reality is Synonymous with Power. And I need to know.

In my funky body mood today I had little flashes of fear. Of her draining me psychically, thinking of me and wanting healing. I also think these little demons are good for me to see.

I look forward to receiving a picture of her. I wish it could be like she looked in the dressing room at 2 A.M. Brigitte, I love you. It would have been really nice to have had all day in the sun to have made love with you, instead of necessarily so briefly.

She really was an incredible lover and friend. It would make me really happy to find out some day that her body is free of the dis-ease. She deserves it.

September 29

Back home in Los Osos now, I feel smooth. Deanne has never looked more beautiful. Kim has never seemed warmer. Rusty never cuter.

I got a card from Brigitte. The first part written in German sounding like Herman Hesse. The whole card was so poetic, loving, and buoyant. And praise after praise for me.

She's back home. She says meeting me was a wonderful experience and wishes she could see me again. Says she'd love to make love with me again. She is so happy. And hopes it can add to her love with her husband; not subtract.

She says I'm the most beautiful lover she's ever had.
Oh my God.
love, love, love

October 2

My loving feels so far away. Brigitte and Sheri. Also my close times with Ancsa, Joseph, Suzanne, John, Bettina, Terése, Susan. They're all so distant. I'm dissatisfied and they're so far away.

It's also kind of like I had such a flood of intimate relationships that one superseded the next and now, away from them all, I realize they were very real but too short to develop that friendship bond. Ancsa alone feels like she's still with me.

October 5

I spent late morning and early afternoon with Deanne. Kim told me tonight I was really special and said, "I love you." Becky called. Joe told me the other night, stoned, after running, as I was standing communing with another runner in the sunset on the cliff, that I looked like a beautiful nymph.

I climbed Bishop's Peak today. I felt strong and alive. Watched the sunset. Home, after showering, wearing just my summery purple pants, I felt so healthy and beautiful all night. I really feel I've gone one step beyond. I've finally gone beyond the routine of our society. Or I've gone there again, this time with the wisdom to share it and use it.

Still, I am lonely. It's different. But my need for a mate feels the same. Sheri alternates between so warm in my heart and vague and distant. Her picture (that I just got) really changed things. Brigitte is very warm and tangible to me. Very close and sustainable.

Maybe this is the time I've been waiting all my adult life for. To have really mature spiritual relationships. To have close female friends again.

I'm ready.

I really feel like I just grew up.

November 4

Once again, back at Harbin.

Typical Harbin day for me. I spent the most of the day lonely and subdued, not talking much to anyone, then things opened up.

I had met Sandra earlier in the day. She is really magical. Napa masseuse. Very sensitive and present. When I went back up to the pools for my last bathing, Sandra was just leaving. She gave me an incredible hug, really held me, kind of surged emotionally, put her hand on my coccyx and pulled me to her. She kind of looked off and had visions. She told me I was about to enter a block of time I can hardly imagine or something like that. She says she sees trees; pine trees, maybe coastal. Then she said, "lots of letting go." That hurt. How much more do I have to let go? But maybe it's just all the goodbyes because I'm so high now, meeting so fast so intimately. I was kind of solemn, I guess, and she touched me with her eyes and whole being and said, "Don't Worry, Little Rabbit."

So yes, tonight I let go or am letting go of two women I could have easily taken home. I really do feel as though I've finally grown up.

The letter I sent to Sheri. First part written September 13th and the second part after getting her letter, September 18th.

Sept. 13, '89
Dear Sheri,
It's been over a week since I saw you drift across the street in Sebastopol with Walt Whitman in your hand. (Lucky Walt)
I have gained a lot of power and freedom and the ability to give more recently by not wanting more from anybody than I can have. That physical reality can't come up to the heart, has evaded me all these years.

You (we) are the ultimate challenge for me, but I think I am almost ready to allow myself to move on in the physical and I hope that will help you become a sweet beautiful memory instead of a sad one.

I am anxiously awaiting your letter to see how you feel. I hope we can continue to write and share ideas and honesty. I want your friendship.

Continued friendship and communication is what always helps me adjust my feelings when the status of a relationship changes. And I hope you will express your needs to me. And doubts and wisdom.

I feel a tickling in my heart now as I prepare to write that I feel a lot of affection for you. I felt there was a kind of grace how we both moved together.

Mon. 18. Sept.

Dear Sheri,

I wrote the above about a week ago and have been waiting to get your letter. I just got it. I hope you are not mad and don't lose respect for me if I admit my need to write you is too big to respect your wish that I don't. After this I'll let it be.

First of all it never crossed my mind that you were using me. And even the idea now is bizarre and alien. Don't feel guilty. That helps no-one. You, me, or your boyfriend. I would rather you were radiant, confident, and believed you had expanded the loving in your life, and now you can bring that home and share it with those you're close to.

I also am having a hard time facing the consequences. Once again in my life I am reminded of what I am missing instead of remaining numb, which I've done most of the last four years. If anyone should feel like they used someone it should be me. You told me that once before you had another outside lover and it caused suffering and still I kissed you. My need to be a lover is so strong that I chose to ignore what would surely be difficult for both of us. I'm sorry, Sheri.

It's been really hard waiting for your letter. I feel much better now. You wrote that you didn't think your letter was what I wanted to hear. I suppose if you had told me that we were to live happily ever after it would have turned me on but short of that I just wanted to hear you talk to me.

I accept your reality. I want you to do what you need to do. You never deceived me. You know that.

As I reread and reread your letter, mixed in with you saying what we can't have, can't be, and shouldn't do, I get over and over again your warmth and affection, and appreciation. I thank you for that and that is what I will remember of you.

It makes me sad that we can't write. But what do I know? Maybe it's best. My way of doing things has never worked anyway.

I do make one final appeal to you, Sheri. Please send me a nice picture of you. I want to remember what you look like and just remember the tenderness. It means really a lot to me. You don't have to write anything with it. I accept you not wanting to keep a dialogue going. And again I want you to know I feel so much affection and caring in your letter that I don't in any way feel you're being mean.

But please would you just stick a picture in an envelope and send it to me.

When I said I Love You to you it seemed challenging to you. I'm sorry. There is a romantic element to it but it is also far broader than that and hey, I got nothing to lose... so... I love you Sheri Dee.

P.S. If you ever feel comfortable communicating with me again, please do.

I may not be very good at doing it, but I do know the Truth.

All you need is Love.
Love your pain
Love your guilt
Love your confusion
Love your boyfriend
Love me
Love George Bush
Love the earth
Love you
Love your loving

Loving, Sex, and Community

Janne, January, 1990

Sebastopol, California

January 25

I've been having a lot of mysterious body pains and discomforts recently. I'm imagining a lot of things, but it is probably just stress.

God, I feel like I need a lover. I mean really need. Almost as much as food and sleep.

January 31

I want a woman so bad.

You know, I think denial is a powerful tool. Your Bushes and Reagans can grow old believing in lies. I can be together and not able to deny the insufficiencies in my life and if I don't make peace with them, I can cause tremendous stress to myself.

And sometimes I just can't make peace with a sexless, romanceless, touchless life.

I think when I was younger and more genitally oriented, I could placate my driving desire by masturbating, by sex with women I didn't have a lot in common with, and by victim orientation.

It seems the more I become aware of my needs as matters of the heart and the responsibility for my own behavior, the less I can satisfy myself, the less denial I can have, and the deeper the loneliness and suffering.

I don't know.

I really liked the guy in Sex, Lies and Videotape who had decided to tell the truth and humbly told people where he was at when they asked. And he asked personal creative questions when he wanted to.

Well... this green ink and these strokes feel good, but it's bed time.

I'm clean and still alive. I've been granted one more day.

February 2

In bed. Sometimes I just feel good for a short space between the awful funky body feelings. After overeating cookies and applesauce, I felt good for a while. Kind of calm and solid. Now, in bed I feel pains and headache.

I've almost cried a few times in the last few days but I just can't seem to get involved or personal enough or something.

I think my grim denial now is exerting tremendous pressure on my body. And I really really need touch. I don't even get many hugs here.

February 3

2:30 in the afternoon.

It's pouring out and I feel good sitting inside, except I feel that if I don't get social, I've wasted a day that might change my life so I don't have to get through another night alone.

February 13

The depression I'm feeling is really intense in its subtleness. I really should be screaming and raving and crying but instead I feel like I'm consuming myself from inside.

I really really really want to totally soak in the joy of the softness and wetness of a woman.

February 14

I just had a wonderful phone talk with Karin in Santa Cruz. I told Karin to look for women who want to have a positive adventure with me when I visit.

I told Karin I hope someday we can be close when I'm happy. I told her people just think I'm not doing so bad because I'm usually healthy and I maintain, outwardly, even when I'm really going through it. She said you'll be happy. I wondered why she'd believe that. She said, "We have to believe in you. If we can't believe in you, who can we believe in."

February 20

Happy Birthday, Janne.

I'm back in Sebastopol after only three days away, but now with loving, sex, and community still warm in my soul. Hanging out with Karin and her neighbors across the street, Janne and I grew closer becoming lovers.

February 21

I'm sitting in the back yard, in reasonably warm sunshine. And feeling a little bit confused. Confused because of feelings about Janne. About the common sense, about her feelings, the reality of it all as it is now, and the fact that she was a wonderful lover and a healthy beautiful body that was so responsive to being loved. She was so soft and wet.

She is so young and the places we are in our lives are not very compatible, so I know now that time will and ought to drift between us and "we" will be past, but I desire the gorgeous femininity of it all. And the togetherness.

As lovers we were really enjoying each other. I really enjoyed the ebb and flow of our talking, playing, tenderness, and passion.

As far as friendship, well, I guess that adds a kind of element of confusion because there is no doubt that our friendship and trust is good; it's only that she was kind of confused and reserved the next day so I had to accept her being more distant. But experience, wisdom, and reality still yield to some extent to gut feelings and emotional needs.

The other sort of romantic thing during my short Santa Cruz trip was visiting Rachel. She looked absolutely gorgeous to me. We talked and it was good for us to see each other again.

I massaged her from behind for a bit then put my arms around her and we cozied on her bed a while and she told me how she feels and felt about me when I was still living in Santa Cruz, except that Joel had clouded the issue then. It was nice to hear her express her desire for me and that she had considered me as a possible lover.

We stood up and she kissed me the wettest softest lip kiss I could imagine. I just melted. Mild torture, but I feel too much respect for her current focus. She felt so soft and warm. A wonderful friend.

It was really good seeing Karin. It was fun with her and nice to be with someone who you can move so easily with.

Their neighborhood community is really nice. Several households open to each other. I feel strongly that it was that community quality that opened the door for Janne and I. A kind of accelerated trust imparted from one relationship to another.

February 23

You know, I should feel a little optimistic. I went to Santa Cruz determined to have sex and I did.

Hello Janne! How are you, love? Things we talked about in between the passion keep slowly coming back to me. Nice to remember how we communicated. I wonder how much and how she remembers us.

I'm in such a strange space of mixed emotions and feelings since Janne. I feel looser, more relaxed, but also restless. I feel somewhat sexually satisfied, yet hunger intensely to be immersed again soon in womanness. I feel more honest and pure in my woman appreciation, yet ache to biological appreciation.

I think of naked time with Janne more than anything else. Her shape and softness and wetness. And her touch and desire. Those moments when I felt so much affection that I'd hold her scalp and a handful of her side or back so hard. Oh God.

March 4

I've had a hard time letting go of sex with Janne. Letting go of her and of us was easy, but the way she kissed and touched, and how wet and sexy she was and how beautiful her body was to me stay with me. Which is kind of strange because I know it was really her friendliness as we were lovers that made her that desirable. I guess that's why I wish she'd communicate with me. We haven't been in touch since I left.

March 6

Today was beautiful and spring like, although still a little crisp to be full blown. Still, I feel spring's biological urge very much. The quality I feel is strong and clear. It fucks me up.

Sitting in my car now, Johnny Rivers' Baby I Need Your Lovin' playing. I haven't heard from Janne and I've felt like not begging or pursuing but hearing this song, I feel like why not?! I want to feel the length of her body next to mine and her holding me and I'm going to ask for it. No need to pretend anything I don't feel. Or couch that desire in friendship games. Shit. Don't I trust my integrity? I want to call and just tell her I want to spend a night with her. That's so beautiful - yet as I write I feel like it's low. Is this where all this growth has gotten me? Afraid to just plain say my feelings?

One other piece of the puzzle is that although I believe it really is a beautiful thing to reach out in and for love, I feel I know psychically and intuitively that she is far too confused to risk another encounter with me. It's just that I would like to not be so certain in projecting separation on our situation.

March 8

I forgot to call Janne again this evening until it was too late. I called earlier and she was at work. I was in the right mood too. Thinking today, I decided if don't ask I'm rejecting myself. Really much more insulting.

March 9

I just met Dory, Salvador's girlfriend, who came over to look at the room we have for rent. She had a wonderful phone voice, and she is as beautiful as her voice.

If she hadn't been Salvador's girlfriend I think I would have to have kissed her.

March 10

I sent a letter to Janne, since I never could get her on the phone, saying I would like to spend a night with her again. I kind of expect no response at all. I think it confuses her and she'd just kind of like it to go away.

And I've been kind of quietly thinking about Dory a lot. I'm not really sure what it is that disturbs me, but I guess it's a combination of things. Desire but knowing I can't have her; envy that someone has her as a lover; and some sort of sense of defeat that women are out there and I'm so lonely.

March 19

I feel deep and lousy simultaneously.

Edgar Cayce, in his readings, talked about "long-suffering." Maybe it's kind of a test - not to be tough - but organically to stick to ideals in an environment that doesn't substantially reward spirituality.

I'm feeling these days that my honesty, my realness, and clarity that I found last fall is alive again and can only get better. It won't be that easy, but I'm going to play and talk and touch and I got nothing to lose but my chains.

Epilogue

I didn't see Janne again until a year and a half later in September. She and I and Karin and Barry spent an evening together. She was friendly, warm, and we four were all so together. When we parted she gave me a deep, long, personal hug that said she remembered and there was love and there was affection.

Aquarian Chemistry

Eileen, February, 1991

Cotati, California

February 17

Debussy's Clair de Lune opened my heart yesterday and today. Really divine. Really divine. Classical music is for me these days like it was for Winchester in M*A*S*H. A taste of civilization and a refined expression of human nature juxtaposed with a world at war and such madness.

I was in a grocery store tonight and the man in front of me had a "support the troops, operation desert storm" T-shirt on. I said nothing but after I left I felt I should have said simply, "Yeah, they can use all the love we can give them."

And realized that with enough love humans can and will make harmonious decisions regardless of what a protester, peace-nik, parent, or president says. Knowing comes.

I hope I have the calm presence and boldness to simply convey a message of love the next time I feel it to share with a support the troops person.

Too much politics.

Not enough love.

February 20

A few nights ago Karen and Cheryl (my roommates) both had lovers over. And they both have several times. I was happy with how it just was as it was and I felt no sense of left outness.

Tonight driving home I was thinking about that and I thought, well, I'm not really happy, I don't feel my life is all that great, I'm not really satisfied with my achievements... but it's my life, it's what I am, and I'm solid. A very strong solid feeling. It's just what I'm doing.

February 21

Just now I was writing to Alain and wrote that I feel like I'm in the center of my Life. I think that's what I was trying to explain last night writing about feeling strong and solid. Perhaps it could better be described as being in the center of Life (without the "my"). Not sure.

February 25

So, yesterday I was really restless. It was a really warm day and I was feeling some springy restlessness, as well as my other war related moods. I worked on some journal stuff a while and kept wanting to be out in the weather but not knowing where. And I had meeting a woman on my mind.

I finally got it together to go to Ragle Park, but noticing how late it was I decided to just go to the Cotati Co-op first and maybe Fairfield Osborne instead of Ragle.

By the produce, in the co-op, I met Eileen. She looked really strong and when our eyes met she really looked at me. She asked me how I was and I explained my war blues.

We talked for a long time about social and political stuff. I asked her to go for a walk and she was playfully open. We went up to Fairfield Osborne. A man with two kids there directed us to a lookout. We sat and watched the sunset and got to know each other.

She was / is very attractive to me but there was / is a little something keeping me kind of in my head. She is an Aquarius. It often seems for me that with Aquarians it is a meeting of the minds. I always seem to get along with Aquarians but rarely feel very close.

Eileen was also holding back a little.

She is 31 which surprised me. She has tremendous wisdom and confidence. And it seems that there is a lot of synchronicity on our paths. She seems to have learned lessons and made peace recently with similar things as me.

We kissed a while by and in the car.

She was reluctant to choose to come home with me and most likely get more sexual. But she did. And we did.

It was wonderful being touched. Many times I'd look at her face and smile and she'd look so beautiful.

We made love a long time in many positions. The attention, the touch, and the loving were wonderful. The actual making love I was a little in my head. But maybe also because she didn't want me to come inside her. So I couldn't let go.

We sort of slept together until she left at 5:30. It was so nice to have her there.

She is here for three more days then goes back to Milwaukee.

She asked me a lot of questions. Sometimes it seemed like too many too fast but they were creative and provocative and I really appreciated her orientation.

I notice as I think about her and us and my feelings that I feel a little guilt about not being in love or overwhelmed with feelings and so on. Like it's an insult to her.

I'm glad I wrote that. Get on with reality. I don't want to perform for her or in order that anything in particular happens with us.

And aside from that I do wonder a little as I sit here by my desk doing journals that I made love last night for the first time in a year and a half and here I am feeling a lot the same as this time yesterday. Not the same mood but I'm pretty much the same me.

It feels right in the sense of being oriented to some bigger picture but also a little scary wondering if I have lost some capability to rush in love and romance.

War news.

My heart is a little aflutter.

Iraqis are supposedly giving up en masse. A new Soviet peace proposal - seems like Iraq will surrender. News that they're already pulling out.

In any case, it looks like the killing may stop soon. That feels good. Beyond that, maybe we can get on with a look at the issues. We'll see.

February 26

Last night Eileen came over, brought my car back which I had lent her, and hung out until I drove her back after midnight.

We took our clothes off almost immediately and made love. She had cleared up some reservations within herself and was more present. She was wetter and opener and being inside her was divine. We move nicely together. It was really hard to have to pull out and compromise the satisfaction.

Talking with her; being with her is so easy.

About her leaving so soon I guess I just recognize that she has things to do in a city and our lives take place in different places. And the fact that I really don't feel romantic seems to make this unattached view easy or easier.

I found myself just wanting sex today at times - very genitally. Wanting to make love, remembering the feelings; found myself looking at women.

At the Morgan Street Co-op I looked very directly at several women and there was some kind of power and purity in it. It seemed they knew I had sex in my life and it was ok to look back at me like they did. It seemed like I was very close to them but I don't think I was. Meaning actually physically, in distance. I had the sensation that we were very close, looking at each other, when, in reality, we were across the room a ways. Just such a presence.

Teresa and sister Sarah were there. Funny, I had been thinking of asking Teresa, if single, to make love with me a week ago. Now I see her. We hugged warmly and kissed soft-lippedly. I got really physically turned on.

February 28

Everywhere women were turning me on today. I felt I could just be wildly promiscuous, really feeling I want to make love again.

Often today I felt again a close direct presence in eye contact with women. It feels powerful, good and clean. It's a wonderful way to look at people. They are surprised and smiling and open usually. It's kind of passing, unattached, and deep and hello. Right into the eye. Amidst other subtle things, that's a really nice side benefit from Eileen's love and loving.

I feel Eileen woke me up. I feel more aesthetic and rounder.

(And the war is over)

March 2

Many subtle residuals from the time and loving with Eileen. I kind of miss her. I feel a continued presence looking at people. A kind of openness to ritual or questing seems to pervade my being, somewhat inspired by her talking of her ways and somewhat by her validation. It brought me out.

During the Doors movie tonight I had to go out and pis. I ran out, ran through the packed lobby. With each person I encountered I immediately took control of the situation and made a move and danced past them successfully before they had a chance to react. I also really connected - briefly - with each one. It was a powerful event.

Later I thought about that as allegory. If someone wants to dance with me at my level they're welcome. When I encounter slower or other, I can be solid and sure in my control - no, in my movement - participating in the event.

March 16

Party here tonight. We fired up the sauna. Teresa, naked, was thanking me for offering her a sauna and rushed a little hug and kiss on me. I instinctively put my tongue between her lips. Eileen kissing naturalness. I remember doing that in Santa Cruz after Jane's and my kissing for days. With Teresa just now it kind of disturbed me. ("Kind of" is an understatement.) I watched her dress after her shower. I really wanted her. Her breasts and belly and... well. It is the most since my changes last fall that I've felt disturbed and wanting to chase woman.

I had a wonderful phone talk with Eileen tonight. I told her how I felt and how I was restless, having been reminded of the pleasure of womanness around me.

I told her it's rained ever since she was here. She said it was our making love. I said maybe we should go on the road, stop the oil fires in Kuwait, end other droughts, and she said "I'd do that." She's great. The war ended the day we first made love. And Northern California's 5 year drought.

A Little Sparkle of Loving

Deborah, May, 1992

Bellingham, Washington

May Day

I just watched The In Crowd. It really moved me. That 60's slowness and sensuousness. Vicki was so heart energy. It turned me on. Dancin' in the streets.

It's like 20 years ago, 25 years ago, at least some people made the best of cities - communing, thriving, concerted energy. Now it's so staid. So mental. And it's just a city. Concrete and machines. Cars and lawnmowers.

Vicki said Dell kissed nice. Soft. Let her kiss back. It moved me.

I long for kissing and lush open hearted tenderness right now. In my mood right now a woman's face seems her most erotic part.

The movie challenged my personal needs now and my choices. My choices as to how I vibrate; from what center(s). My choices as to what I appreciate.

There were many qualities portrayed in people in the movie that I appreciated but that wouldn't satisfy and would disappoint me now in real life. Hollywood silver screen perfection dreams vs. real choices of our will and what we are capable of imagining and manifesting; actually doing - today - here.

"With which of your qualities do you want to catch a woman? Because it is those qualities, most likely, your catch will match. Validate your most valued side and attract souls that recognize that."

May 22

Before bed last night I read some of Right Use of Will. Essentially, about "all-loving" being fine, but the Will must be engaged to allow all feelings to move out, no denial, and allowing the Spirit to become a fully sentient open vital part of God again.

The book inspires me to be all loving.

Curious thing though. It urged one to express and let out all emotions... but don't impose it on people who don't want to hear it.

Exactly my dilemma, it seems. I'd love to let it out, but I don't feel I've been given permission or urged by one single being in Bellingham to do that.

It seems I am facing an essential problem/possibility of trying needing to love with no one to share it with. Just love. Just know it's still the best thing there is. Undirected, even. It seems that directed involves too much hope to share it.

June 8

I went to a woman named Deborah at Passages book store today, and got a 45 minute psychic reading. Beautiful, light, loose, good.

She is very attractive to me. I didn't say that to her but after the reading I asked her if she was single. She, smiling, said not married but quite connected. Then she said, "You're very attractive too." We hugged. Nice hug but short, she being a little cautious. We broke our hug and kind of held hands a little.

We walked out and talked. Just before goodbye, she leaned down to me (she's taller and I think I might have been a step down; not sure) and kissed me a soft loving lip kiss. My reaction was deep and obvious as I said, "Wow." She agreed in energy and body and was kind of shy. We said goodbye and parted.

I haven't yet made a separation, really at all, except for the mental decision that it must be so. My heart is tingling.

June 9

I made peace with our situation quickly but that little touch of heaven that descended upon me still holds a charge. Somehow, how the kiss was so unexpected and how soft her lips were and how she leaned down to me really made it feel like it was a gift straight from heaven above.

I'm turned on. I've been charged all day. The most physical charge I've had in ages. I'm kind of thrilling to this growth the way I used to all the time in Santa Cruz. Even before Deborah I've been feeling like just asking women to kiss, really kiss a moment just to add some special pleasure in our days. Feeling really clean and righteous in the purity of the act.

And now... And now I'm aching to see a woman's face while I'm deep inside her. The face that it seems can't possibly exist when you see the face people wear when they mope around in a stupor through their city days (daze).

June 22

Right now. What I'm feeling.

Appreciation, in general, and also disturbed because of facing my ego-centric world view. And the vicious circle of my aloneness compelling me to be pickier and pickier.

I just spent some time with Deborah again. I went to Passages and found her between readings. Immediately she was so sweet, stroking my hair, commenting on my jewelry. We talked a while and she asked me if I wanted to come back and go for a walk after her last reading.

I did and we did. She asked me why I came back to see her. I told her I wanted a friend but probably wouldn't have if there had been no romantic energy.

She was just as honest. She has two kids and lives with a man in a stable happy but not completely emotionally or sexually satisfying relationship.

I explained my Prince Valiant tendencies and we discussed priorities. I saw this neat picture of a spectrum of issues that are probably the same for everyone but we stack them differently.

She says she asks herself about her needs sometimes but is happy.

I believe her.

She asked to get together and what I'd like to do. I said beyond inappropriate intimacy, I'd like to listen to music or do anything in nature.

I believe she is happy but I feel also that she is attracted to having a little sparkle of love energy in her life.

Talking with her I felt really appreciated and also self conscious of my critical nature. I left our time together feeling a little muddy. A strange mixture of exalting in my world, my summer, and my life opening and expanding and feeling the burden of my distance from pure loving.

Well..., time, space, and matter. Life on the planet.

June 24

I'm at Boulevard Park. I feel emotionally kind of crummy.

Deborah came over today, this afternoon. She let herself in and came to me and sat with me on my bed.

We talked in the kitchen a while and she said at one point, "Why am I here?" I asked her why and she said "escapism."

Back on my bed we laid and listened to On The Threshold Of A Dream. She was warm, close, and pretty aggressively got close to me.

We eventually made love.

Before we made love, lying naked together, I asked her, "Why are you here?" She said, "to fuck you."

I pretty much knew how much she wanted me, but because of the situation, I assumed nothing. I never did ask her how it is with her in light of her being "happy" at home.

So why do I feel crummy?

Thinking about feelings. Trying to recognize the source. Some possibilities:

• I knew she had to leave soon and I, having already had an orgasm in her mouth, wasn't really quite emotionally ready for making love; I was pushing it.

• I didn't come in her and wanted to. It felt a little incomplete.

• I feel kind of too fast alone. I was really loving her touch, kiss, skin, self, company.

• I never completely let myself into it knowing she has her life and I'm a fling.

• And, maybe the simplest and most profound reason why I feel crummy. Because I'm feeling. It's like I feel (a little, just a little) like I could crash and just feel lonely and cry; really cry.

I really loved her. She kisses like I like to be kissed. Soft and hard and everything in between. And I really loved all of her. Kissing her pussy was wonderful. I felt like if I had had all day, I would like to have lingered and lounged between her legs for a long, long time.

I felt in love with her face. I loved looking at her and being close.

Funny thing. I don't feel sexually satisfied. Because I didn't come in her? I don't know. Maybe just because I want a mate, a companion, someone to stick around.

(Between June 25th and June 28th I went to a "Healing Gathering" in Eastern Washington. While there I spent a couple of days together with and fell in love with Lori. Something very powerful and deep was happening between us.)

June 30

I called Deborah today and she had free time and came over. She asked me about my weekend. She had alluded, on the phone, to her feelings being an issue and I insisted she tell me first about that. She is seeing that she is slowly facing her feelings and acknowledging she has emotional needs that need to be met. Being with me brought it up.

I told her about Lori and she was sincerely very happy for me and also felt very left out. We sat and laid together for a long time. She cried a little. At times she expressed she was mad at me.

It was intense and beautiful. We talked about our chemistry and my feelings of being sexual with her while "in love" with Lori. I said it's not the act, it's the energy I would carry away from the experience that makes that not right for me right now.

We kissed a little. She is truly a wonderful kisser. We have tremendous chemistry. But kissing her, I knew I couldn't be present.

It was really hard for her. She whispered "I love you" in my ear. Curiously, I barely heard her and thought she said "goodbye." And it seemed not like she was leaving but like goodbye to one phase of us and hello to a new.

I felt longing for her, love for her, and did, in fact, feel sad and sorry we weren't making love but still couldn't imagine - could only kind of see how hard it was for her.

I made sure she knew I was available if she needed to talk or share with me. She oscillated between wanting to see me and feeling like she won't want to because it would hurt too much.

Just before she left, she just took me and kissed me hard and we kissed for a minute or two.

I felt really blessed to be given an opportunity to love this woman and be capable enough to help her and allow her to feel.

I felt so warm and full after I was with her.

July 27

Deborah just dropped in. Messed up my bed a little. At one point I lifted Deborah off my bed and she just swooned. She said she gets really turned on when I do something with my strength.

Maybe that's something really important for me to remember. I am so feminine and gentle in some ways that inside of a woman's trust I can be a strong male. Maybe outside too. I don't know. Maybe physically inside their trust. And in unneedy confidence outside their trust.

My body loved Deborah's visit. Caresses on my butt and legs and kissing. I do have a kissing relationship with a woman.

Epilogue

Deborah and I stayed friends. Years later, she would call me in California and tell me she was going to be doing a workshop at a nice retreat spot in Napa County and would I like to get together after the workshop was over. It was unspoken but both of us knew we had arranged a sexual tryst. We made love and had a nice reunion.

Finding Resolution Alone

Lori, June, 1992

Living in Bellingham, Washington

As mentioned mid-Deborah encounter I went to a "Healing Gathering" in Eastern Washington between June 25th and 28th, where I spent a couple of days together with and fell in love with Lori. She lived in Seattle.

June 26

I met and sat with Lori by the sauna. We went in together and without her glasses she asked for help. It felt like velvet holding her hands, leading her in. I sat with her, led her out, did it all again. She was so easy to touch so I said to her that I found it so easy to be close to her that I wondered if I should be cautious or something like that.

She said clearly openly truthfully that was ok, she's used to getting close to people fast, and would let me know.

I walked her to her tent, hugged her, and we kissed.

Magic was/is afoot.

I had asked her if she is single and she said yes, forever. Why? Because she's hard to date. Why? Because she's psychic and knows what men are thinking (or feeling). What am I thinking? She described a kind of humming like bopping along. How nice!

I have never felt so clearly in love. Really, never.

I love how she reads me and likes it.

She had to go off to do fire watch. She knew I was afraid of losing her. She assured me she wasn't going anywhere.

She is so soft and sweet. She is half Eskimo and half Danish. Her affection reminds me of the movie, Eskimo.

No more now. I'm almost afraid of myself. I can't be good enough or open enough or flexible enough to be present and be beautiful.

She was full of gentle compliments.

Just before we parted I was rubbing her head with mine but thinking far away. She said you're thoughts aren't with what you're doing but I still like what you're doing with your head. My God.

June 27

Well, I finally got the cry out that's been building up for 2 years. At least, some of it.

Laurie refuses to let go of the pain of a dysfunctional upbringing, and holds in contempt her past life deaths and feels sentenced to purgatory on earth.

That's her cover and not all of her believes it. I know that.

She needs lots of alone time and says she can only be single.

I cried hard facing that this woman is not anytime soon going to spend much time with me. And I don't like the idea of hoping, thinking I'm putting energy into and making choices that will bring us to a point where she feels differently.

She has chronic fatigue syndrome. I asked her if she knew why and she said yes, because she doesn't want to live, but they won't let her go.

Her hating life is the line she needs to hold onto while she grows.

She has just left. Within minutes, I began to feel that I can love today. I look outside and feel that I can bring some grace to these people. My heart is maybe as strong as I have been beginning to believe it is.

She is the straightest, most cosmic woman I've ever known. She is so clean.

Sex last night was the best sex I've ever felt. She has never chosen a creative capable man as a lover before. Says she's never been cried on before.

I don't know if I have, plain and simply, chosen another completely unavailable woman or if I've met someone who I can grow and learn with and must simply accept that I must accept the whole package.

I know that was the Yolanda trap. There are differences. This woman isn't lying to me and saying we will, in time, be together. And this woman is not connected to another man.

There are also similarities.

Away from her now, I know just one thing. I can't count on her. I really can't. I just have to keep all of my love alive and watch what happens as I feel through time.

I wonder if Deborah and Lori are openings as I become so rich in my capabilities. It's kind of odd to think of being close to someone else now, though. Although as I write and think that, I see and feel that as an old Scorpio game. Maybe I can go out and love, be my lover self that I feel is so easily me now.

Later - In my tent alone. Today felt like about 3 days long. I mean that literally. It was so long. Lori and I kind of came together on and off all day. We never were sexual today. I kind of wanted to be but I think it was more that a part of me wanted evidence of her wanting to share that with me.

But, also, as the day progressed, I felt more and more good about us. Not confident of any outcome. But I believe it's good. And I'm capable of loving as we do or don't do whatever.

She suggested for our first tryst, whenever, going to the Olympic Mountains.

I sure don't know how any of this will play out, but there are possibilities.

She is an extremely dynamic woman.

She is unpredictable but her integrity and goodness are true.

June 28

I'll go home today.

My thoughts about Lori are confused. She doesn't and never will (I think) fit any picture of a rosy couply relationship. Somehow as I mature my unique desire panoply, that is fitting for me.

Yesterday the little Russian boy, camped nearby, came over and visited me and hugged me goodbye and kissed me on the face. Then a few minutes later he came out while I was at my car and he walked with me on to the bridge holding my hand really sweetly.

I also got high helping a little girl wash her hands. She couldn't turn the spigot and kind of frustrated pouty called out "I need help!" I was hacky sacking nearby and went and helped.

Later I ran into Gretchen. She was so soft and warm and I really liked her. She was teasing and easily talking about feelings and group energy and personal things. I gave her a really good back massage. Afterwards she did me. Really good once I let myself into it. She felt really altogether sane and attractive to me.

Later - I opened my tent flap and looked out at the tents and trees and thought to myself, I feel like I could cry. And I did. It's been a long time since I could cry so easily.

I found myself crying and laughing, reflecting on Lori, on my life, on the people here. I got some heart rushes on love for Lori. Since crying, I've been lying here for a long time, drifting in a state of appreciation.

I had some beautiful feelings coupled with recognizing the rightness of Lori's individuality and seeing no reason to have her fit my pictures.

Other times in my history I've come to this in radical mood swings needing adversities sweet milk, but this is different. More natural and validated, not just by a knowing, but by the fruit of experience having seeded itself through winters of change and having blossomed in the spring of a new and improved me.

- - -

I've been feeling really mellow during my time here, kind of groovin' around in a state of grace. At the sauna, I encountered Karen, Lori's new friend. She was going through changes and I helped her by talking, listening, and touching her. We had a nice connection.

Leaving, as I was driving out I saw a woman walking, from behind. Before I saw her face, I thought, this woman is really beautiful, I wonder what she looks like. It turned out to be Regie. I got out and we hugged. She was wearing a cotton summer dress and I really felt her body. She is so gorgeous. At the end of the hug, I put my hands on her hips and she felt so incredible I said something like, you really feel good, and hugged her again. We talked a while and it was really good.

God I've been touching all these women with all this love energy in me. Yesterday I kissed Gretchen's ear. She was surprised, then said, "I guess I can trust you."

Lori left me a note on my car. She called me Blue Eyes, like she did so sweetly before. God, what a rush. And she wrote "So good to find you." Not "meet you," "find you." She is so far out.

July 11

It's been two weeks since our magical coming together at the Healing Gathering and I'm off to Seattle to see Lori. I don't feel that I'm blindly rushing over there to recapture the magic of that weekend. It's just that some of the mystery will come to pass. I would love if magic is still afoot between us but I don't go in hopes of convincing her of how she ought to want me or with the idea of proving to myself that she's the one. Little parts of me; ancient character traits want that two dimensional silver screen simplicity, but there's not much chance of True Love flourishing that way.

Synopsis of visiting Lori in Seattle.
(Not a journal entry.)

I visited Lori in Seattle and she threw up walls immediately. The Healing Gathering and me had been for her an escape from her normal life, and she had no inclination to be so free with me again. Our visit was, at first, nightmarishly cold, then she warmed a bit and her affectionate Eskimo nose rubbing side shone through, but we weren't going to be. And she wasn't going to participate much in us at all.

- - -

The rest of the Lori encounter is not journal entries listed by date but different writings of some heavy personal reflecting in the following weeks.

I felt so unguarded at the Healing Gathering with her. So free. Then in Seattle and since I feel that it would be so easy to make big mistakes. The joke is that I must be unguarded or what is it worth. Like being free of other's judgment. I wonder if it is still dragging me that I feel that I'm insufficient because there's ways I act that are bad. Also, related, I feel sometimes that I am responsible for her not wanting to see me and that I blew it; I blew the good male role model opportunity. I didn't do any thing that horrible;

wanting to get to know parts of her life; how should I know they were supposed to remain locked away. I'm doing my best to learn from what I did do and I'm just not that bad. I need to revalidate my love of self; not to stand up for myself against her (or anyone's) opinion, but just because I must to be true to myself and validate myself so I'm capable of functioning.

I was thinking about how I had the feeling Lori was reprimanding me; telling me I must find all in myself. That seems true and absurd. What a wonderful paradox. If all is found in self the self would open to recognize itself as a part of all.

It seems the joke is to look for all in self. Except that we are so literally into self, our bodies, our lives, that we have nowhere better or closer at hand to look. But when we become freed of and beyond astrology, our parents, our karma we simply share space, energy, love with other beings as one.

- - -

I've been thinking about Rusty asking me if Lori had acknowledged at all, her role in our relationship's big shift in Seattle. No, I don't think she did at all. She just acted like I was intrusive and faulted to want something of someone else.

And I was thinking about her asking me to hold her a great portion of the time and being vulnerable and wanting me to express my love and desire for her.

It struck me that there is a kind of real life action principle here that maybe will help me understand and help me deal with expectations of others, particularly in intimate situations. Lori speaks her own truth very well. She says what she feels and what she knows and actually "is" at the moment. But when another person comes into the picture (me, in my case), then it is acts, not words that speak our truth.

An individual's own truth is how it works for them. What they know they need or want. It's their psychology and the safe protected place they have made regarding their sphere of concerns.

But with another, those safe places are challenged and the simple (well, not simple, but recognized and "used to") truths don't have much to do with how that individual will act.

Lori did want to be held and loved and in love, but when she felt insecure in my desire and need, her acts were responding to other things.

For myself, I think this means that when someone says to me they want something with me, I must recognize that that might be their truth they are speaking, but they can't really know how that truth will stand up under the conditions of needing to share another's style.

Of course all of this is relative to several things.

• How much a person has tested being close to others and learned they can still be themselves.

• How much a person has done individual spiritual work to develop the confidence that they can be flexible and still maintain their safe places.

• And mostly, how much a person has outgrown the need for safe places, coming closer and closer to being psychology free and history free, being able to stay in loving when in the presence of new and unique influences; being able to stay in creativity when in the presence of new and unique influences. Right now that seems really important.

Each little god must know that sharing and being open with and to another little god cannot impede their creativity; their ability to create their own universe.

In fact I see this fitting with my True Love rap. The clearer and freer each little god is, the less their creativity is threatened by another's, and the higher the potential is for the two (or more) little gods to co-create fearlessly and joyfully, giving up nothing with everything to gain.

What does this mean for me personally in terms of being still apparently a relatively fearful and lonely creator (lover)? It means that I hope in future comings together I can recognize that without a woman (anyone, really, but the charge is usually higher with a lover and when wanting something we look at people differently) intending to deceive me, when they tell me their truth, their desires, wishes, what they want with me, that I can, without being cynical, expect the acts to be different as their safe havens are challenged by my style, my vibrations, and my needs.

- - -

Neediness?

Lori said needy energy is muddy energy. I think she's right. She sees it psychically. I feel it. But also during my walk it came to me - there are no victims. In any "relationship" both parties have responsibilities. Nothing specific, just that they are participants. And if one finds muddy energy coming at them, especially in an outwardly consciously chosen relationship, they have the potential to behave both physically and emotionally and spiritually in such a fashion as to raise the situation.

Why does neediness become muddy energy? It really doesn't have to be. So many times my neediness has been a beautiful human moment of sharing. With Boehr, for example. And many times, as with Deborah, I have been on the other side and nurtured the other person and we have had an opportunity to grow and help neediness be a vehicle for loving and unity.

So, what is it? It is the guilt. And where does that come from? From without. From buying the pictures of parents, society, or anyone whose approval you need or who you give away your power to. It's all related to not loving yourself unconditionally.

Lori has tremendous guilt around neediness. To her it is practically a sin. She is thoroughly convinced that in life she will be hurt if she needs anything from anyone else. She hates and won't forgive her mother for not meeting her needs. She avoids the whole thing (not completely, on all levels, but that's her movie) and projected the guilt on me. My presence and especially my desire to get to some of the roots so that we could make peace threatened her safe haven so she headed that off at the pass and projected "it's bad" onto the whole thing between us. Which, in itself wouldn't create muddy energy. Just that I bought it because I wanted to be like she wanted me to be and wanted her approval.

Also, people in denial are usually very solid in their belief; these beliefs are very crystallized and have not yet been allowed light that would threaten the safe haven. Consequently, they can be very convincing.

And again, on the psychic in denial of feeling theme, it's like the energy I used to feel at Berkeley Psychic Institute. The energy is kept (clairvoyantly) clean by avoiding feelings and as long as everyone buys the paradigm, it's solid.

What needs recognizing, as I see it, is that the needy energy that is being felt is not really the essence of that individual. And it can and will change.

I want to be around people who aren't so needy that they are afraid to be needy. I have been "accused" so many times of being needy. Outwardly, yes, I am. But that is because coming together is prioritized for me and I'll take the occasional groping, if need be. The people who have accused me of being needy are people who are so needy that they avoid it altogether by getting stuck in dysfunctional and dishonest relationships that are stable and by getting into distractions like business or attachments to society standards that validate survival-oriented achievement instead of personal and consequently interpersonal growth and spiritual loosening.

Now, there is a whole new can of worms. The concept of survival-oriented achievement. It really explains the world of business and money and politics. That was, in fact, perhaps, the biggest core issue that blew the generations apart in the sixties; what people wanted validation for. Growth and value oriented achievement or survival-oriented achievement.

- - -

I feel like this state and these levels I've come to is manifesting in a grown up world of real and honest concerns and issues and involvement with good capable people questing for truth and understanding.

Epilogue

Sometimes when I'm longing for contact I think there must be a myriad women who tonight wish they also weren't sleeping alone. Although that must certainly be true, one can't expect just any two people to come together and satisfy each other. Which is to say, that if I find a woman attractive, I can't expect her to want me also, just because she's lonely. But... there are enough of us to satisfy each other and what is at the heart of this, I believe, is that people ought to ask for what they want and share their inner selves, their desires, their hopes, and their pain. I believe the rest would follow. We are indeed all in it together. Custodians of each other's souls.

I believe that in a natural society with joyous, free, spontaneous, creative people, people would receive enough loving. Men and women would flirt, play, and come together easily. In between, or perhaps among, magical relationships of duration, men and women could kiss, could stroke each other, could praise each other, and could make love to each other. With clarity and good intentions various levels of closeness happen naturally.

I feel that if one always knew that loving and appreciation and touch and sex weren't far away that we wouldn't distort our perceptions to satisfy our need to feel loved or to pretend anybody is more than they are.

Of course, this requires participation. Both with each other and with ourselves.

Not having attachments doesn't mean not having commitments.

Without having all your eggs in one basket you can love each other for what you offer in real functional life - not fantasies.

So... I believe in this. And why doesn't this happen? Very few people are ready for this, which is simply to say they can't imagine it. I can. And I feel in light of this that finding and/or creating a community or circle of people who desire this is very important to me.

Not a frivolous free love sex society, but a commitment to owning our feelings and owning our emotions. Also a climate where people feel safe to take emotional risks.

To allow the heart, which I believe knows only truth, to lead.

More Thoughts on the Love and Sex Dance

a few more relationship related journal entries

I think sometimes about Kay and Jerry telling me of the letter from Sharon telling of how happy she is, of how caring and warm I am. What would a letter say now? Why don't I seem to be happy enough or easy enough to give enough?

She cares so much for me and really wants the best for us. She knows how loving I can be but is now living without much loving support from me. Myself I could say the same thing about. Maybe I've fallen out of love with myself. Maybe if we could wait to fall back in love with someone else like we do with ourselves. Or if we had to, like we do with ourselves.

- - -

A few days ago I went into the bookstore and was instantly attracted to a woman I saw. She was looking at records in the pile next to the Brahms I had come in to look at. Being close to her I felt her energy really strongly and clearly. There was no wondering if I was imagining it. One word came to mind. That I was experiencing and standing within her fire.

- - -

In spite of all my philosophy, I hunger for Susan's beauty, remember her touch.

As much as it hurts, as I entertain leaving it behind and vibrating at a higher level, I know I like it, I want to feel lonely. There's something rich, earthy, and human about it. Something sweaty.

- - -

Being positive seems so simple, why do I want to be in pain? I guess this is just an awkwardly shaped block I've got to carve into shape and fit into my ever widening foundation.

- - -

Hypothetical situation: two people meet, happy with themselves and are happy to find they can share their own happy lives with each other. From that point on how do they ever know if they could or would be happy apart? And does it matter? Is it determined by how content they were alone before they met?

It seems what's important is they just have to know when they're together that they're doing what they want. And if they never find out, the reason why they won't is better than the answer.

- - -

Maybe what's happening here is that my head doesn't miss Jane (and it really doesn't) but my body's intelligence does. Jane and I shared so deeply. My energy feels naked, so to speak.

- - -

I had this dream during relationship struggles:

A baseball game. One team had been ahead but it all fell apart in one inning. My teammates were down because of it but resigned and philosophical. I was in the field but without a mitt. Not in a position or really on the team. I handled the ball a couple of times. I consoled them; said they shouldn't feel bad, the terrain was so rough. It was wild hilly, rocky country, not a baseball field.

- - -

I slept with Cathy last night. It was nice being with her but I wasn't all there and felt guilty. Just now as I sat down to write I realized what I did last night. I withdrew from loving because I feared the responsibility. It required that I communicate to Cathy how I felt. Perhaps had I not withdrawn, that alone would have made it clear. Or perhaps a few words from my heart. As I was almost asleep I felt myself slip into a euphoric state as she caressed me. What a shame that it took until my mind and walls faded.

- - -

Gyanda and I talked about dynamic people in a relationship and how patterns and rules don't work; how you need flexible dynamic attitudes and based on real inner things. She said about patterns and rules, "it's dangerous, you can fall asleep."

- - -

Maybe it's just - and I mean Jane and Sue, Mary, probably others - that when there's a breakdown in the flow I start to see the games and "good reasons why" exposed in resistance and I want to get into it. I want to talk and explore and the other person is like hey, I didn't want to get into this level, let's forget it and stay where we were.

And I can never go back.

- - -

I was thinking about Dorinda and why I'm not completely free in my appreciation and loving of her. My last feelings of her were disappointment in what either I perceived or Claudia conveyed of her current situation being a compromise of her power and brilliance. I've let that cut me off from her. Not good. "She" is still the same and her heart and soul are to be respected and loved.

Reading in old journals about my three weeks in Copenhagen sleeping with and sharing a room with Lene and being so clear and loving, I wondered why I don't have now a warm glow when I think of her. Then I read of how jealous and possessive and even obtrusive she was a month later in France regarding Sarah. Again I have lost the core for an event, a moment.

I read in my journals so many wonderful glowing things I said about Tafay during my time between Europe trips. It surprised me because now I hold a memory of somehow being down on her. I suspect my sexual frustration and our communication issues.

I really need to come back to the goodness and the smiling faces of these people of my past. Remember their hearts and know whatever flaws in them or perceived or imagined by me are transitory.

Especially with women I think I can be disappointed because I wish them to fit pictures of mine because I'm still wondering where out there satisfaction for style like mine lies.

I just have to love and look forward to opportunities to smile wholly on these old friends and mean it from all my heart.

- - -

At the health food store this afternoon I was passed closely by a really attractive woman. I reached for her eyes and said hello when I got them. She said hello and I asked how she was. She asked me and turning her head, held a smile eyes as she passed.

- - -

Darcy has much insight and native wisdom. She was talking about relationships and about how they grow, come to fruition, seed, and die. And they will live again. In another life or time. I got how even each phase, each new energy has its flow and is expended. Remain true, remain friends and honor each new energy. And not only cycles, one after the other, but longer and shorter cycles overlapping.

- - -

I'm having warm thoughts of Darcy today. Like I have some curious sexual energy and desire playing off my loops about relationships. Each time I have a feeling different or less than the infatuation I seem to desire, or maybe the fall I desire, it quietly passes away and I feel the goodness of knowing this woman. Her sensitivity and good nature. Her humor and strength to be what she feels to be in her heart.

At one point today, while working, I was thinking of sex with someone else. Kate. And the old picture of me freely loving many women came up. Really loving and sex.

In that moment it seemed absolutely equally as pure and whole as sex with one woman. In fact the quality is all that matters. It seemed then absurd in my mind that people have pictures of frivolousness and dirtiness if you say I made love 10 times last week... with 5 women. And their pictures are of tenderness and in love if you say I made love 10 times last week... with one woman. Also in that moment I realized how I was still buying into that guilt.

I feel so capable.

I feel no ill will towards anyone.

I feel so much to share so much love and affection.

I feel, in such a simple straightforward way, what I have to give.

I feel Darcy and Kate both are happy to have me catalyze openings for them.

- - -

Interesting how we hate parts of people we love because those parts blow our perfect pictures. Why waste time and energy hating those parts. You've just got to adjust and accept and perhaps, if there's an agreement to grow and help each other, it can be something delved into together.

But wait a minute. That sounds great, but isn't that just the reasons relationships don't work. One or both partners is or are protecting their pain and won't let down the armor. Or, how about this; for one of them, exposing certain facets is not threatening and they expect the other to be able to explore that area too, while for the other, that pain, that lie, that encrypted movie drama is not slated for deciphering yet. And vice versa.

- - -

I didn't plan these fantasies. I only observe.

I don't understand waiting. What is there to protect? Let's make love with affection, Laurie. Let's let love flow through our bodies. Supercharge. Or at least sleep together. That alone is a mating. Not so challenging but such a communion.

But can I wait a day to see Laurie and get this off my chest.

Working in the shop is a nice rhythm today but it seems so foreign. Like Shane looking down at the shovel in his hand, in wry amusement of his current occupation in contrast with his true calling. Why this option? Today I play the craftsman.

Looking at Shane now, yes, so many levels of the human equation. The integral force when necessary or possible. And yet the physical demands and the karmic and personality pressures compelling.

That old feeling. Wanna go, far away. Just go.

Step on the gas and wipe that tear away.

- - -

I was thinking some today about the quote from Starseed Transmissions, "You began to carry over past patterns of behavioral response into new relationships. This made you less effective in those relationships because you were no longer fully present, no longer using the fullness of your potential."

Thinking about the post Jane days. It can be very difficult to be unattached and difficult not to want to protect oneself from hurt. But you don't know you're going to get hurt. In fact, you can't get hurt without your own permission. Sure, when things change in a relationship it's hard and confusing. But I think it comes back to the same lessons I learned from Yolanda. Is the other person willing to participate? At what levels? If not or not enough, then well, I guess you're not mated. Personal requirements play their role. Time, attention, willingness to conceive of ideas, etc.

If it just isn't functioning (subjective) then get high again, love life. And enter into each new relationship with child-like excitement. Don't carry over responses and expectations based on past relationships. The only thing the same in a new relationship is you; and you have the power to be free of past patterns.

- - -

It was the Love in Action Fair today in San Lorenzo Park.

A beautiful soft people loving day. It started for me feeling low. Kind of quietly solemn. That changed. The last half of the day I felt high and it was easy to tell people and show people the beauty in themselves.

Earlier, I had met Daney and we talked and kidded and shared special eye contact. I pursued her in the manner of hanging close to her and talking, very forward about liking being with her and she felt fine with it. It was the most I've felt easy light playful desire for a woman in a long time.

Of course, she is leaving. To S.F. tonight, Arizona tomorrow, and Mexico next week.

I played with talking her into staying knowing we just had to smile and let it be.

It warmed my heart to have let myself love as I did. It was so good the parting didn't hurt. Doesn't hurt.

Lying on my back, at one point, I thought, oh well, there's so and so reasons we wouldn't be close, then caught myself. Great realization. I don't need to bullshit myself so I'll feel ok about not being with her. Reality is synonymous with power. She's leaving and we shared and it was and is good and the alternative future didn't happen. It is good.

I think that was the point my day changed.

- - -

It seems that ever since I've begun to write down clear headed glimpses of the insanity of this relationship, that after each realization, figuring out, understanding, or objective perception, I would not let myself just put the pen down and let that be its own animal and sink in. I would always have to say one more thing about missing and needing, and bring up the hope fantasies of a future for us; a thread to hold onto. Like it would be sacrilege to acknowledge her weaknesses and inabilities to satisfy me, and my strengths and knowing, without also giving weight to the vision of usness and her goddess-like stature.

- - -

Coming back to the debate about the importance of "practical" life pursuits vs. emotional relationship life pursuits, I believe that one should be able to have their heart wide open and feel good about everything. If keeping the heart closed is required to appreciate or focus on aspects of life, then I believe it is a mental decision. If opening the heart brings up emptiness and brings up sadness, then that should be responded to. Just look at how lives are structured. Most wake hours are devoted to work and errands and organization. A couple of hours maybe to being open to feeling even if one has a lover or intimate friends.

On the other hand, if love's needs are not being denied, then when the heart is open other aspects of life will be joyful and be seen in a wonderful light and won't be tasks.

The heart must be the bottom line. No, maybe not. But it must at least be allowed its fare share. Not a token feeling once in a while.

- - -

I can't and never will be able to change anyone. I know that but it's just always a shock to me that people will be so high connecting at their core and not seem to care to strive to stay there. And when I get so close to women in the honeymoon phase, I can't believe they wouldn't choose to ask each other for help attaining a continuous loving state.

- - -

With her boyfriend, Holly's choices seem so limited. If their relationship was healthy, she could grow, challenge her limits, and feel feelings for and with others. Otherwise reality is denied; the script is rewritten to accommodate a weak actor.

- - -

Observing J and J's relationship I see how they have roles and patterns they expect each other to fulfill. It's painful for me to observe and be around. They argue about things that aren't the issue and tease around challenges to each other. They insist each other perform and do what they have come to count on for validation and to maintain facades. It's like when the relationship developed they made unspoken contracts about how it was between them and now they are bound by those contracts. When either of them don't get from the other what they thought they had procured in the deal, there is conflict.

- - -

I realized with stunning scary clarity today how most men must feel to women and why it's so hard to be a natural loving animal and not scare them or encounter walls.

Today I had a temp job tearing a roof off of an old water reservoir out in the woods, working with repulsive men. Each break and at lunch I had to walk far enough away from them so that I couldn't hear the sound of their voices. If I was a woman I wouldn't want to allow any part of the energy from men like that into my space. It's violent, ugly, demeaning, and dominating.

So when I look right at a woman and when I say biology or sex or I like you with my eyes or energy, how many women are willing to take the chance to even let down their shields to find out that it is gentle and loving.

And today for the first time I guess I really understand the scope of the risk.

Possibly this comes to me also in the light of beginning to have some perspective about how hard it must be for those who have grown up with screwed up parents to take risks and to try and live up to higher ideals and desires.

- - -

Intense sexual longings at Harbin Hot Springs yesterday. The most in a long time. I felt that familiar feeling of wanting to know a woman through her body, through her sexuality and being subject to her choice for my happiness. A strange visitor from the not so distant past but I have profoundly changed enough so it seemed odd. Still, I haven't integrated new attitudes enough so that old appeals don't confuse a little.

But each of several women who were really attractive to me (beautiful bodies and sweet faces) passed out of my life almost as fast as they passed out of eyesight and physical presence (though I still remember them).

It's like when you make an impression in the vinyl on a massage table and it resumes its natural smoothness only in time; the impression slowly fading.

- - -

It seems sometimes that women are offended by men wanting them. I want and try to give something and they act like I'm trying to take something away.

I just realized that yes I want to give but anytime I lose confidence and give into needing or anytime I let a woman's fear shift my needs to wanting something from her, even if it is just completion or clarity, the energy begins to flow the other way and she feels it and I am indeed, trying to take something from her. Not away from her. I don't have that power. But fear comes with the energy changing directions.

It really strikes me how important it is to keep free loving flowing as much as possible, outpouring towards my brothers and sisters. And to be aware that when I fail to do so, that others will tend more to fear my drawing energy back towards myself.

- - -

Time is a major factor in developing a bond with another so that a person will feel like they want more. Time to trust, or sometimes the trust is already there, but time to become enveloped in a feeling that they want to continue.

I think women particularly, when men are trying to get closer to them, require more time usually to scope out the situation. And most people require more time than I do to feel comfortable going further or deeper. Fear and caution play a bigger role.

Second, I think often I feel rushed to invite someone to a more personal opportunity because I don't like how the small talk is or where we are at the time. It could be by a street, at a loud dance, or any of many places I find obnoxious or compromising. Unfortunately these places also serve the function of protecting against intimacy. And slowing things down.

If I could sit and prattle on the cafe's balcony over the obnoxious traffic for an hour with someone it might evolve into suggestions of something / somewhere / sometime else together, but for me that is torture. It is physical torture, psychic torture, and the reasons disappoint me.

And another factor. How many women have I developed wonderful loving relationships with organically as friends or housemates who I'd love to make love to, us already having the communication and trust and duration of friendship down, but they can't make love or be physically intimate with a friend. Which brings up my thoughts on what it really is that creates chemistry. I'm really beginning to believe that it almost invariably involves and requires a certain amount of loose ends and antagonism. I mean that in a pure sense; not necessarily implying outward disharmony. There are karmic implications and parental implications; the theory that people seek out mates to prove they can get love from a situation where they failed to before.

I feel I can love and love deeply without the antagonism (though, admittedly, that has been the most compelling). And I feel I would now seek the assurance that in finding love I don't need to prove myself against historic patterns; rather that I am sufficient as is, and seek love and loving and intimacy with women with whom I share clarity and a sisterly love.

- - -

Relationships begin when people are in sympathy at some level. It is naive or perhaps just plain stupid to think the original sympathy will remain. So often I have been with women in their strength, in their hearts, and in their bodies, and have assumed these qualities to be normal to them.

In fact, in many, maybe most cases the strokes bring out strengths and beauty that isn't normal. It seems clear to me that honesty, open attitudes, minimal attachments, and a commitment to full awareness are necessary to shift and stay in love mode.

Furthermore, it seems that instead of fearing falling out of the original sympathy or withdrawing when it does happen, it can be viewed as an opportunity to get on with the inevitable: the discovery of other sympathies. And learning to sustain caring and validation for the process during the time in between.

Of course, this requires that both people be willing participants and are dedicated to honesty, acceptance, and full awareness. I would suggest that the commitment to these ideals be expressed verbally.

Even if you're not talking about mating forever, if hearts are open and intimacy is desired, it's good to talk of these things. Essentially, I do want to know about forever. Not necessarily mating, but a love and respect free of or with a minimal amount of left over entanglements.

- - -

It's a viscous circle. I really believe that one of the worst most devastating things about being single so long is that you don't smell like sex at all and women aren't interested. They might even meet you, know you, are around you, but you're just a nice guy. You aren't the man they want. It's most likely not even conscious.

- - -

Something struck me today in its ultimate simplicity. Sure, men and women want the same thing. It's just that women want to first connect, be cared for, build some faith, then be more physical. Men want to dive in with blind Aries energy, connect physically, have sex, be satisfied, then mellow and expand to caring, deeper bonds, and shows of faith. Women want the softness to lead to intimacy while men want the intimacy to lead to softness.

It's just kind of an out of syncness that's built in to push us to go deeper.

- - -

Yesterday Gina and I met up at Ragle Park to play whack-it. We hugged when we met and she really hugged me, much closer than we ever have before, with an intimacy we have never had as friends. After playing we sat and talked. After a while I took her hand and when I kissed her she kissed back. We talked and kissed for a long time. Afterwards, walking back to the car, we were holding hands and she felt like my girlfriend. What a wonderful feeling. I remember sometimes I have called men's wives girlfriends and they've corrected me, seriously proclaiming Wife, like it's so important. You know, I don't know if it gets much higher that the feeling of having a girlfriend. To me it connotes a playfulness and youthful spring like feeling.

- - -

I have felt spring outside me this year but today was the first time it penetrated. I am spring today. But I think that's the very reason why loneliness has been striking me so deeply. I'm infected with The Wind In The Willows' spring's "spirit of divine discontent and longing."

Sex didn't cross my mind before or after being in town today, but while I was there, I found female forms striking deep chords. Something like the feeling of fresh berries. Luscious.

Music Appendix

Below are words from music that appear in the journal excerpts, in the order that they appear. There may not be the exact words as they are sung or were written. Listed underneath each is the person or group that performed them.

Everything is broken up and dances.
    - Jim Morrison

I let my woman flow to her own natural rhythm.
I let my woman flow to her own natural rhyme.
    - It's a Beautiful Day

People who need people are the luckiest people in the world.
    - Barbara Streisand

Who in the hell d'you think you are? A super star? Well, right you are!
    - John Lennon

Wouldn't it be nice. If we could say goodnight and stay together.
    - The Beach Boys

With a lover I could hold my head back and really laugh.
    - Joan Armatrading

MacArthur Park is melting in the dark...
All the sweet, green icing flowing down...
Someone left the cake out in the rain...
I don't think that I can take it...

'Cause it took so long to bake it...
And I'll never have that recipe again.
> \- Richard Harris

Freedom is the lesson we must learn.
> \- Elton John

My love is burning like a forest fire.
> \- The Moody Blues

Out of college, money spent. See no future, pay no rent. Oh, that magic feeling. Nowhere to go.
> \- The Beatles

The difference between me and you
I won't argue right or wrong.
But I have time to cry.
> \- Crosby, Stills, and Nash

And though my life was filled with wonder, my heart still knew some fear.
> \- John Denver

Magical connection
Genuine affection
Parallel direction
In between the lines
Why!?
Why try to be otherwise!!??
> \- John Sebastian

Made only more painful by the knowledge that all that I am is of my own making.
> \- Procol Harum

I'm getting tired of saying do you come here often.
    - The Who

Lay down beside me. Love ain't for keeping.
    - The Who

Who among you will run with me?
    - Jim Morrison

The song is over.
I'm left with only tears,
I must remember.
Even if it takes a million years.
    - The Who

Once there was a way to get back home.
    - The Beatles

pent up aching rivers...
    - Not sung but the words of Walt Whitman

About the Author

I was born in Seattle and spent the first 30 years of my life in the Pacific Northwest. Well, except for 4 school years in a private Quaker boarding school in Pennsylvania, which was a great communal living experience. I think this had a far reaching and profound effect on my life. I have since lived in many different places, mostly favoring the West Coast; Olympia, Bellingham, San Juan Island, San Luis Obispo, Santa Cruz, Santa Fe, Maui, Kauai and currently Sebastopol, California. Integral in my experience has been a number of trips to Europe, mostly spending my time in the area around Innsbruck, Austria, which is my second home and where I have so many dear friends.

Work has also been varied; most of it being for myself. I have worked as a carpenter and with a partner built 2 houses in the mountains (one in Idaho, one in Washington) using (almost) exclusively hand tools. In Santa Cruz, I started my own business building and selling portable massage tables of my own design and did that for many years.

I love music; my favorites being classical music of the more sublime nature (Debussy, for one) and psychedelic era rock of which I consider the Beatles to be the ultimate. My favorite instrument is the human voice. Music has been a cornerstone of my life and has carried me through many peaceful and turbulent times.

I love to get out and ramble around on my mountain bike. It keeps me young; not the exercise so much as the playfulness and freedom of it.

And my most recent passion is playing strategic eurogame board games with friends.

Other Books by Roger Golden Brown

The Truth Seeker's Handbook has been published in print and as an eBook. I kept journals for over 20 years, writing almost every day. Much of the philosophy, the struggles leading to learning and the attitudes that helped me get through life appears in this book. It has a section dealing with major life themes, one about our relationship to the Earth, one retelling stories of serendipity, and finally a section of reminders to help along the way.

Two of those sections are available as their own books:

Themes of my Life

Reminders From Life for Life

Excerpt from The Truth Seeker's Handbook:

Delight in truth at all costs. We really must accept everything we experience. Simply say, yes, this is happening to me. We tend to avoid and repress and choose against less pleasant feelings. What a rip-off! They offer powerful information as to what is going on; information as to the reason why we don't at the moment have pleasant feelings. The desirable feelings validate flow and rightness. The unpleasant ones are the ones needing the most attention.

- - -

Insights has been published in print and as an eBook. This is a compilation of most of the journal entries which didn't appear in any of my other books, but that I felt needed to see the light of day. I organized them into such categories as Cosmic, Philosophy and Attitude, Love, Society, and several more.

Excerpt from Insights:

I heard Earth Angel on the radio today and thought about the American Dream and its surfacing in the 50's and the dreamy songs reflecting it. I was overwhelmed with a rush of rightness. Sure it is distorted. Sure its means are destructive. But the dream - to have comfort and ease and the time and space to relax and expand, time to create, to have comfortable homes is fine. It sparked a spiritual movement which unfortunately was complicated by an awesome opportunity to be corrupted by material and sensory numbing diversions. But the dream itself, it's not only the American Dream but a soul's dream. To mellow a life in a body. To find harmony. I'm all for it.

- - -

Heading Out is poetry and prose and has been published in print and as an eBook. Cryptic and cosmic might be good words to describe these writings; word adventures. Poetry is an individual thing and I can't say for sure you will like them, but look for it and check out the free eBook sample.

A short poem from Heading Out:

> Popsicle process brings freedom ... in heat.
> What was ice yields a watery treat.
> When we allow ourselves to have what we need
> That water fertilizes and brings life to our seed.

- - -

33 Years of Dreams has been published in print and as an eBook. Over a period of 33 years I wrote down a ton of dreams. A friend once said to me, why would anybody want to read anyone else's dreams? That got me to thinking but it came to me you could also ask why would anybody want to read anyone else's poetry? They are the same, in a way; kind of cryptic non-linear stories that take images and create something to be interpreted. After trimming out some of the uninteresting and poorly transcribed dreams it is, in its final form, almost 700 pages and is published in 2 volumes. They are for sale individually.

A dream from 33 Years of Dreams:

I was with a pet, female, smiling Buffalo and a group of friends hanging out in the country. And with an alien friend who materialized to be with us. There was a river scene, after going through a gate. Rednecks were hassling us, then we saw three of our women being physically abused down the road a ways, by three men. We headed down in force (with our alien and Buffalo) to deal with it.

Where to Buy the Books

To buy the books in print go to my Author Page:
http://books2read.com/rogergoldenbrown

Versions of these books in eBook format can all be found at Smashwords, as well as free sample downloads:
https://www.smashwords.com/profile/view/Rogue17

Check out my Smashwords author interview here:
https://www.smashwords.com/profile/view/Rogue17154